Romans: Empire and Resistance

T0353234

Romans: Empire and Resistance

An Introduction and Study Guide

Sze-kar Wan

t&t clark

LONDON • NEW YORK • OXFORD • NEW DELHI • SYDNEY

T&T CLARK
Bloomsbury Publishing Plc
50 Bedford Square, London, WC1B 3DP, UK
1385 Broadway, New York, NY 10018, USA

BLOOMSBURY, T&T CLARK and the T&T Clark logo are trademarks of Bloomsbury
Publishing Plc

First published in Great Britain 2021

Cover design: Charlotte James

A catalogue record for this book is available from the British Library.

A catalog record for this book is available from the Library of Congress.

ISBN: HB: 978-0-5676-9349-5
        PB: 978-0-5676-7503-3
        ePDF: 978-0-5676-7504-0
        ePUB: 978-0-5676-7505-7

Typeset by Integra Software Services Pvt. Ltd.

To find out more about our authors and books visit www.bloomsbury.com
and sign up for our newsletters.

To the young people of Hong Kong
who dare to stand up to an empire

Contents

1

How to Read Romans?

Paul, a slave of Christ Jesus, called to be an apostle, set aside for the good news of God that was promised beforehand through his prophets in holy scriptures concerning his son who came out of the seed of David according to the flesh, designated Son of God in power according to the spirit of holiness by resurrection from the dead, Jesus Christ our Lord, through whom we received grace and apostleship for the obedience of faith among all the Gentiles, for the sake of his name, among whom you yourselves are also called to belong to Christ; to all God's beloved who are in Rome, called to be saints. Grace to you and peace from God our father and Lord Jesus Christ.

(Rom. 1.1–7)[1]

So begins Paul's letter to the Romans, the last of Paul's extant letters but also his longest, written in the last third of the fifties of the Common Era. The movement of which Paul was a part venerated a man executed by Roman authorities in Judea as a rebel agitator, one Jesus of Nazareth. But instead of staying in the backwaters of Judea, the movement made incursions into the Mediterranean world by establishing meeting cells in cities around the Empire. Such a transgressive move beyond its traditional borders had its challenges, not the least of which was how to deal with the incongruity of touting someone who had been crucified as the long-awaited messiah. Crucifixion was the 'most extreme form of punishment', typically reserved for enemies of the state and slaves;[2] the Jewish messiah, at least in popular imagination, was expected to deliver his people from tyranny, and it was

---

1 Unless noted otherwise, I am responsible for all translations.
2 *Summum supplicium;* Cicero *Verr.* 2.5.168. Crucifixion was ranked higher in severity than decapitation (*decollatio*) or burning at the stake (*crematio*). See O'Collins (1994: 1207).

assumed that the deliverance would be executed through military or political means. This incongruity escalated infinitely when Paul, self-designated as an apostle on behalf of just such a messiah, now decided to write to the meeting cell in none other than Rome itself, the seat of the very empire that crucified Jesus. How he presented, then resolved, this incongruity underlies his Letter to the Romans.

At the outset, I want to emphasize that Paul was not a Christian but a Jew. It would be anachronistic to call him 'Christian', of course, for Christianity had not yet become a sociologically identifiable group separate from Judaism, and Christians did not begin adopting the title for themselves until the second century. More important, though, is evidence gleaned from Paul's own statements that betray a robust confidence in his Jewish identity and upbringing in Judaism. He calls himself a Pharisee and claims to be a scrupulous follower of the Torah and its stipulations, so much so that he pronounces himself 'blameless as to righteousness under the law' (Phil. 3.4–6). He also tells us that he is 'zealous for the traditions of [his] ancestors' and that he is steeped in them far beyond his contemporaries (Gal. 1.14). There is no indication that he did not remain a faithful Jew throughout his life, even after his call to be an apostle to the Gentiles (Stendahl 1976; Eisenbaum 2009: 132–69).[3] If that is the case, Paul's purpose in writing Romans, or any of his letters for that matter, is not to start a new religious movement; he is much more concerned with an internal reform among his own kinsfolk than with creating a sectarian group. The starting point for that reform is what God has done in and through Jesus, who was appointed Christ and the cosmic Son of God at the moment of his resurrection (Rom. 1.4).

Reading Romans Politically

As is typical of his extant letters, Paul's self-introduction hints at how he wishes to relate to his intended audience.[4] In Romans, he introduces himself as a 'slave of Christ Jesus' (1.1). That is not necessarily a title of self-abnegation, however. In light of the destination of the letter and the theological-political overture of the prescript to be discussed below, it should probably be taken

---

[3] It goes without saying, Paul was never 'converted' to Christianity if Christianity had not even existed as a religion separate from Judaism. See Segal (1990) for a detailed discussion.

[4] Obvious examples can be observed in Gal. 1.1; Phil. 1.1; Phlm. 1, and so on.

as a title modelled after the well-known 'slave of Caesar', who was a member of the imperial household serving as personal representative and occasional emissary of the emperor. Archaeological evidence and inscriptions paint a picture of someone whose direct access to the emperor gained him power and status denied to all but a select few (Jewett 2006: 100). A slave of Caesar spoke no words of his own but only on behalf of the emperor, though reality was different. 'Given that his master was a son of a god and his word was backed by the full power of the Roman military establishment, the slave's word would be a powerful medium indeed' (Brown 2004: 733). In calling himself a 'slave of Christ Jesus', therefore, Paul presents himself as a representative of Christ, an emissary tasked with conveying not his own but the words of his master, 'the good news of God' (1.1).

The title 'slave of Christ Jesus' enables Paul to make a subtle claim for Jesus. In contrast to the Roman ruler who calls himself a 'son of god' (*divi filius*), Jesus is the Christ, the Son of the true God (1.3–4). 'Christ' has lost much of its political connotations through centuries of domestication, but it is the Greek translation of the Hebrew *mashiach*, 'anointed', a title commonly applied to kings and royal figures in biblical tradition. So King Saul is called the 'anointed of the Lord' (1 Sam. 12.3, 5, etc.) in biblical parlance, as are King David (2 Sam. 19.22; 23.1, etc.) and his successors (2 Sam. 22.51). True, Paul does not always attach full messianic significance to the title 'Christ'; his writings betray no urgency to demonstrate Jesus is the Christ, and nowhere does he use the common expression 'the anointed of the Lord'. Nevertheless, for Paul, 'Christ' applies uniquely to Jesus and is therefore defined by him and not the other way around. So for Marinus de Jonge, 'The designation "Christ" receives its semantic content not through a previously fixed concept of messiahship but rather from the person and work of Jesus… When early Christians spoke about (the) "Christ", they meant Jesus in whom they believed; they did not necessarily intend to convey the "messianic" connotations of the term' (de Jonge 1994: 915). That said, Paul is well aware of the messianic significance of the title. He lists 'the Christ coming in the flesh' as one of the prerogatives of the Jewish people (Rom. 9.5) and calls Christ 'a servant of the circumcised for God's truth, in order to confirm the promises of the patriarchs' (15.8), thereby connecting 'Christ' to messianic expectations of old. Here, in his self-introduction that opens the letter, he vests 'Christ' with full messianic force by juxtaposing it to 'the seed of David' (1.3), which is a royal title heralding the arrival of the Davidic messiah in the end time.

Paul gives himself a second title, 'apostle' (1.1). An *apostolos* was an ambassador representing an authority figure in communicating his or her wishes to other lands (Herodotus 1.21; 5.38, etc.). When Paul joined the Jesus-movement as a latecomer, *apostolos* had already developed into an exclusive title for leaders in the emerging hierarchy. In his polemical letter to the Galatians, he claims the apostolic office for himself, for he feels he is as entitled to it as the so-called 'pillars' because of the commission he received directly from the divine (Gal. 1.11–12, 15–16). In denying the Jerusalem leaders the exclusive right to the title, Paul in effect tried to return it to its original meaning as a representative of God. The related verb *apostellein* ('to send'), after all, referred to being commissioned by a divine authority; Epictetus called a wise man 'apostle', because he was sent by Zeus (Epictetus, *Diss.* 3.22.23). In introducing himself to his audience as an apostle, therefore, Paul signals his intention to extend his position as member of the inner circle to that of a divine ambassador, '*set aside* for the good news of God' (Rom. 1.1). This language is identical to his self-description in his polemical letter to the Galatians: 'When [God] who had *set me aside* from my mother's womb and called me through his grace was pleased to reveal his son in me, in order that I might proclaim the news of him among the Gentiles … ' (Gal. 1.15–16). Then, as now, Paul highlights his divine commission to preach the good news to the Gentiles.

To modern ears, 'good news' (*euangelion*) is safely consigned to a piety divorced from the public arena. To first-century ears, however, *euangelion* was part of an extensive vocabulary associated with the emperor cult, which marshalled religious symbolism to facilitate governance of the empire. The cult depicted the emperor as an extraordinary man embodying good fortune, salvation, even divinity. His birth, accompanied by cosmic signs and power and portended by other astrological wonders, was proclaimed as 'good news'.

When Paul says he is charged with preaching the 'good news of God' (Rom. 1.1), therefore, he has in mind the identity of Christ that stands in stark contrast to the imperial propaganda of Rome. (See Chapter 3 for a more thorough discussion of 'good news'.)

This reading of *euangelion* is consistent with the political-theological intensity of the self-introduction (Taubes 2004: 13–16). The good news has to do with '[God's] son who came out of the seed of David according to the flesh, designated Son of God in power according to the spirit of holiness by resurrection from the dead, Jesus Christ our Lord' (Rom. 1.3–4). 'Seed of David' is of course a political term, but it should be understood in light of

Paul's apocalypticism. According to the Psalm of Solomon, the messiah will come out of the Davidic line and will restore Israel to its former glory: 'See, O Lord, and raise up for them their king, the son of David, at the time which you chose, O God, to rule over Israel your servant' (Ps. Sol. 17.21 Atkinson). Restoration of Israel's fortunes would take place when the nations (read: *Gentiles*) are defeated and brought to justice: 'The reign of our God is forever over the nations (Gentiles) in judgement' (Ps. Sol. 17.3 Atkinson adapted). The expectation that the messiah will subjugate and judge the Gentiles finds a ready echo in Paul's understanding of his own mission. He describes his apostolic responsibility as demanding 'obedience of faith among all the Gentiles' (Rom. 1.5). The meaning of 'obedience of faith', a phrase unique to Romans and repeated twice more (15.18; 16.26), will be discussed in the next chapter, but it refers to Gentile submission to Christ Jesus (Elliott 2008). A similar scene is depicted in Daniel's dream, in which the human figure (Son of Man) is appointed to rule God's elect with humaneness and justice, while foreign powers are defeated and held in judgement (Dan. 7.1–14). In other words, this messianic figure proclaimed by Paul is no mere human ruler; he is a king after the ancient Davidic line 'according to the flesh' (1.3) but is consecrated as the Son of God through the resurrection 'according to the Spirit of holiness' (1.4). It is this dualistic conception of Christ as flesh and spirit and his divine appointment that set him apart from all self-appointed emperors. The heart of Paul's *euangelion* consists of 'the affirmation of Jesus as the traditional Davidic Messiah, who was adopted and enthroned as the Son of God on the basis of his resurrection' (Jewett 2006: 104).

'Son of God' as a royal title can be amply documented in biblical and extra-biblical sources (e.g., 2 Sam. 7.14; Ps. 2.7; 89.26–27). The coronation psalm, 'You are my son; today I have begotten you' (Ps. 2.7), was central to early Christian articulation of Jesus. The Gospel of Mark, for example, uses it to define Jesus's messiahship (Mk. 1.11). The title is also found among the Dead Sea Scrolls: 'This is the assembly of famous men, [those summoned to] the gathering of the community council, when [God] begets the Messiah with them' (1QSa 2.11–12; see also 4QFlor 1.10). Less studied in modern times but far more prevalent than Jewish usage in the first-century Mediterranean world was the use of title by Roman emperors. Upon coaxing the Senate to declare his adopted father Julius divine (*divus Iulius*), Augustus declared himself *divi filius*, 'son of god'. This title was proclaimed on diverse media around the capital, but none as popular and effective as coins struck with that title. Seen against the background of Roman political theology, Paul's well-chosen titles for Jesus no longer look so innocent.

It has been suggested that Paul's presentation of Christ is influenced by popular images of the emperor (White 1999: 130–2), but it might be more accurate to say that Paul intentionally marshalled symbols and titles from his own ancestral traditions to present a King Jesus who stood in direct opposition to Caesar. As Dieter Georgi concludes, 'If the terms chosen by Paul for his Roman readers have associations with the slogans of Caesar-religion, then Paul's gospel must be understood as competing with the gospel of the Caesars' (Georgi 1991: 87). Proof can be found in Paul's depiction of the sonship of Jesus that follows a Jewish apocalyptic pattern. Christ acquires his title Son of God not by self-acclamation but by divine demonstration of God's power over life and death. Christ's resurrection is a forerunner of the general resurrection when the hoped-for peaceable kingdom of God is about to be realized. The valley of dry bones in Ezekiel 37 played a significant role in shaping popular expectations for the end time, but it was the book of Daniel, composed under the dictatorship of Antiochus IV (167 BCE), that explicitly raised the spectre of the resurrection:

> There shall be a time of anguish, such as has never occurred since nations first came into existence. But at that time your people shall be delivered, everyone who is found written in the book. Many of those who sleep in the dust of the earth shall awake, some to everlasting life, and some to shame and everlasting contempt. Those who are wise shall shine like the brightness of the sky, and those who lead many to righteousness, like the stars forever and ever.
>
> (Dan. 12.1–3 NRSV)

The assertion that a messiah would be installed through the resurrection had no precedence in Jewish literature (Collins 1995: 104). Paul had integrated the apocalyptic expectation of general resurrection into the Son of Man tradition of Daniel 7 in response to a pastoral issue in the Thessalonian congregation (1 Thess. 4.13–18), so in all likelihood, Paul himself, not some early creed, was responsible for making this breakthrough.[5] Such an interpretation allows him to transform a local kingship into cosmic rulership. In the felicitous words of Anton Fridrichsen: 'Through His resurrection

---

[5] As with many commentators, both Jewett (2006: 104) and Hurtado (1998: 95) think Rom. 1.3–4 is a Jewish messianic tradition that Paul cites here for effect. That hypothesis attempts to fit a 'primitive adoptionist' Christology into a supposedly 'more advanced' doctrine of pre-existence but is unnecessary. These categories were foreign to Paul, and the putative tension between these two Christologies dissolves once we note that Paul is more concerned with presenting the seed of David in terms of his Jewish apocalypticism.

from the dead, Jesus, formerly the Messiah of the Jews, has been enthroned as Lord and Saviour of the whole world' (Fridrichsen 1947: 10).

Ever since the Reformation, Paul's letter to the Romans has been read as a handbook of timeless doctrines. Philip Melanchthon famously called Romans a 'compendium of the Christian religion'. Even today Romans is commonly read as Paul's systematic theology that supposedly proceeds from universal sin to solution in Christ (one prominent example is found in Dunn 1998). Such a proposal accounts for the seemingly systematic appearance of the letter, its irenic tone missing in his other letters, and its pattern of developing earlier themes (e.g., body of Christ, 'the strong and the weak', Adam Christology, Abraham, circumcision, the law, etc.). Given the high concentration of political-theological terms used in the opening verses, however, and the multiple ways these terms stand in opposition to imperial propaganda, it becomes increasingly untenable to read Romans as an academic tractate detached from the capital's political and theological agendas. It would be an anachronism to impose a post-Enlightenment separation between politics and religion on a reading of an ancient text – let alone one that was consciously composed to mimic, then oppose, the political and theological language used exclusively by the overlord of the very imperial seat of power to which the letter is being sent. Rome, after all, was well known for manipulating religious symbols to maintain *pax Romana*. In coins and such visual aids as dioramas, sculptures, triumphal arches, and so on, the Romans proclaimed themselves as the authors of peace and benevolence. In their own self-understanding, it was Rome's divine mission to govern the peoples of the world and to impose upon them the rule of law – that is, *Roman* law. In *Scipio's Dream*, General Scipio's grandfather appears to him in a dream to foretell his decisive victory over Carthage that would establish Rome as the undisputed master of the Mediterranean world. In the dream, Scipio tours the heavens and is told that the Empire is founded and ruled by heroes whose true home is in the heavens:

> Be assured of this, so that you may be even more eager to defend the republic. All who have protected, aided, or enlarged their fatherland have a reserved place prepared for them in the heavens, where they may enjoy a beatified existence forever. Nothing accomplished on earth is more pleasing to that supreme God who rules the whole universe than human associations and councils in justice being bound together, which are called states. Their rulers and protectors come from here and thither they return.
>
> (Cicero, *Rep.* 6.13)

This pronouncement is presented as 'prophecy', disclosed to Cicero's readers in an otherworldly journey identical to those found in Jewish apocalyptic writings, thus giving this political agenda eternal legitimacy. In accordance with this vision, it is Rome's foreordained destiny to extend its borders to incorporate others and to impose its law, forms of government, civilization, and indeed its 'peace' (*pax*), upon the world.

In Book 6 of Virgil's *Aeneid*, the rise of Rome is again presented as prophecy to be etched into the history of time. The dead Anchises takes his son Aeneas, Trojan hero and legendary founder of Rome, on a tour of the underworld and introduces him to all the 'future' heroes of the Empire. This prophecy thus establishes, in apocalyptic prophecy, Rome's entitled domination of the whole earth and all its inhabitants:

> Roman, remember by your strength to rule
> earth's peoples, for your powers are these:
> to pacify, to impose the rule of law,
> to spare the conquered, to battle down the proud.
>
> (*Aeneid* 6.851–53)

By contrast, Paul presents to his readers the good news of God that stands in stark contrast to the imperial counterfeit. The good news is couched in traditional Jewish terms: prophecies of the holy scriptures, the spirit of holiness, traditional Davidic messianism, and victory over the nations. It is expressed also in terms unique to the early followers of Jesus: Jesus having been raised from the dead, the general resurrection, and the imminent kingdom of God. Even though these categories might fall into what moderns call 'religious', the gospel's political dimensions are also unmistakable. The good news of God consists of the announcing of the new regime and proclaiming of the newly appointed king, the cosmic Son of God, and Paul has been commissioned as the new ambassador to convey it to all nations. Readers of the letter could not have missed the reference to the imperial propaganda, because it intrudes into their lives daily. Later apologists for the Roman Empire certainly understood the political significance of these words. Melito of Sardis, for example, noted the contrast between Christ and Caesar in Romans but insisted that the two were distinct but complementary 'saviours' of the world (Eusebius, *EH* 4.26.7–8).

As a counterweight to imperial propaganda, this letter should therefore be read as a form of resistance. By 'resistance', I am not suggesting that Paul had even hinted at armed revolution; nowhere in Romans or in any of his surviving letters do we find evidence of Paul ever advocating violence.

Instead, Paul formulates his resistance by excavating his ancestral traditions buried deep in the sediments of the prophetic past. So, the good news of God 'was promised beforehand through his prophets in the holy scriptures' (1.2). With the help of scriptures and tradition as interpreted through his apocalypticism, Paul constructs an anti-imperial discourse in which God of the Jews, through upheaval, will triumph over all earthly authorities. Through the death and resurrection of Christ, the end time is already breaking into the political arena inhabited only by imperial aristocracy. In Paul's conception, the Jewish cosmic vision, according to which underclasses of the Empire will be elevated from their lowliness and rulers of worldly regimes will be humbled in a long-awaited reversal, is about to be realized (Wan 2000a). One of Paul's goals is to lay a theological foundation for setting up Jerusalem as the centre of an alternative kingdom of righteousness, a kingdom in direct competition with Rome. Paul does not intend to make Rome his own domain (Käsemann 1980: 397; Jewett 2006: 923–4), not so much because he refuses to build on someone else's foundation but because he is convinced that its centrality is being replaced. Paul might have learnt his empire-building impulse from his imperial masters, but he surpasses them by constructing a new script of sweeping cosmic scope.

The Congregation through Roman Eyes

The imperial authorities made an impact on the Roman congregation in another way, albeit indirectly. According to Luke, the oldest record of the event, 'Claudius had ordered all Jews to leave Rome' (Acts 18.2). Among the exiles were Priska and Aquila, whom Paul met on his founding visit of the Corinthian congregation.[6] The edict was probably issued in the year 49 CE, early in the reign of Claudius; Luke is otherwise silent on the cause for the expulsion. The Roman historian Suetonius, writing in early second century, added more details: '[Claudius] expelled Jews from Rome for constantly disturbing the peace at *the instigation of Chrestus*' (*Claudius* 25.4). Chrestus, a common name for slaves, is probably a misspelling of

---

[6] Luke introduces the couple in the order of Aquila and Priscilla, with Priscilla being a diminutive of Priska (Acts 18.2), but subsequently as 'Priscilla and Aquila' (Acts 18.18, 26). Paul calls Piska by her proper name and introduces her as the leader of the duo in Rom. 16.3 (Lampe 1992).

Christus, since both sounded identical in the first century. In a report on the Neronian persecution, historian Tacitus made the same mistake by calling Christians *chrestiani* (*Annals 15.4.4*).

Suetonius's note leaves ambiguous whether in fact all Jewish inhabitants had been ordered to leave Rome or had it affected only those involved in the disturbance. According to Roman historian Dio Cassius (c. 155–235 CE), Claudius did not banish Jews from Rome but only shuttered their synagogues, because it would not have been practical to expel such a large population:

> As for the Jews, who had again increased so greatly that by reason of their multitude it would have been hard without raising a tumult to bar them from the city, [Claudius] did not drive them out, but ordered them, while continuing their traditional mode of life, not to hold meetings.
>
> (*Roman History* 60.6.6)

Some argue that Dio's account is referring to an earlier event, but several considerations would suggest he has here the Claudian edict in mind. First, if this notice referred to a different event, it would beg the question why Dio would pass over the Chrestus-event of 49 in silence when its scope would be broader and its punishments harsher. Second, the insistence that Claudius did not expel the Jews reads like a correction of Suetonius's account. Third, if the Jewish inhabitants of Rome had increased to the point of making wholesale expulsion impractical earlier, the condition would hold true in 49 as well. Finally, Luke has a tendency to single out Paul's role in the founding of the Corinthian congregation, and that might have led him to exaggerate the scope of the expulsion to minimize the contribution of Priska and Aquila (Lampe 2003: 11–12).

Dio's account makes no mention of the cause for closing down the synagogues, but the increase of the Jewish population hints at successful proselytizing that brought a large number of converts into the synagogues. An increase of Jewish inhabitants prompted Emperor Tiberius to expel Jews from the capital in 19 CE (Dio, *Roman History* 57.18.5a). If we believe Suetonius that the disturbance in 49 CE was caused by 'the instigation of Chrestus', it seems hard not to conclude that it was the success of the Jesus-missionaries that was responsible for the sudden increase of Jewish population (Jewett 2006: 18).[7]

---

[7] Feldman (1993: 304) agrees that Dio referred to proselytization but does not entertain the possibility that it was carried out by Jesus-missionaries.

A fuller picture now emerges from these three accounts. Only leading figures such as Priska and Aquila thought to be responsible for perceived disturbance in their synagogues were sent away from Rome, but the overall scale must have been small enough not to be regarded as expulsion by Dio. The exact nature of the disturbance remains uncertain, though both historians laid blame, wittingly or unwittingly, on the success of missionaries in bringing Gentile into the Jesus-movement. Synagogues were ordered closed as punishment, strongly suggesting they were the centre of the Jesus-movement that precipitated the disturbance. This sudden influx of converts so filled the synagogues that it must have appeared to outsiders as an increase of Jewish population.

Conversion to Judaism carried a heavy price in Roman society because of its social stigma and costs. According to Tacitus:

> The other customs of the Jews are base and abominable, and owe their persistence to their depravity; for [they are] the worst rascals among other peoples, renouncing their ancestral religions, always kept sending tribute and contribution to Jerusalem, thereby increasing the wealth of the Jews... Those who are converted are to despise the gods, to disown their country, and to regard their parents, children, and brothers as of little account.
>
> (*Histories* 5.5.1–2)

Converts to Judaism were considered Jews and might have carried additional financial burdens as well.[8] They did not necessarily lose their citizenship as it was possible to be Jewish and Roman citizens, and many were. In times of crisis, however, their loyalty to Rome would be severely questioned and they could suffer the same fate that befalls born Jews. As converts to Judaism, they would be suspected of violating their sacred duty to *pietas*, which meant loyalty to Roman tradition, religion, and family.

Many Gentile followers were probably drawn from the ranks of Godfearers, 'the pious of the nations of the world, but not part of the holy people, the people of the Covenant' (Taubes 2004: 20). They were enamoured of Judaism for its high moral values and participated in the synagogue but had not submitted themselves to the full rigour of conversion. The Jesus-movement must have proved attractive to them, because it promised full status in Judaism but did not require circumcision, a rite of passage that

---

[8] The infamous Jewish tax (*fiscus Judaicus*) was imposed on all Jews and converts to Judaism throughout the empire, but it was instituted only after the destruction of the Jerusalem temple in 70 CE, and Jews in Rome who were non-citizens would be taxed as other resident aliens (*peregrini*).

would open them to social isolation and legal jeopardy. Judging by the way Paul uses the term 'Gentile' in Romans, his usage does not deviate from convention and is entirely stereotypical. He distinguishes Gentiles from Jews by the usual restrictions, with circumcision being the most visible rite of passage. All this coheres with the picture painted by the Roman historians, that the synagogue was the centre of activity for the earliest Jesus-missionaries, all of them Jews by birth, to carry out their proselytizing work. Once instigators such as Priska and Aquila were deported from Rome, their absence left a vacuum in the fledgling Jesus-movement that was quickly filled by the Gentile followers of Jesus.

The Neronian Persecution of 64 CE gives us a glimpse of the Roman congregation fifteen years after the edict of Claudius and about half a decade after the writing of Romans. According to two accounts, the Roman authorities rounded up 'Christians' and executed them by gruesome yet legal means on the trumped-up charge that they had started the great conflagration of Rome on account of their hatred of humanity. That Christians were identified as such on their own and not as a subgroup of the Jews speaks volumes that followers of Jesus were by then distinguishable from Jews by their signature gathering, rites, and customs. The edict of Claudius had evidently set in motion a withdrawal of Gentile followers from the synagogue to form their own distinct organization.

One can also deduce from the severity and scale of the execution that the majority of Roman followers of Jesus were not citizens but resident aliens (*peregrini*). According to Tacitus, the condemned were wrapped in wild animal skins to be ravaged by wild dogs, crucified, or burnt at the stake for night-time illumination (Tacitus, *Annals* 15.4.4; see also *1 Clem.* 6.1). The sheer number of such extreme executions and the relative efficiency with which they were carried out make it unlikely that these Christians were Roman citizens. Roman laws would not have permitted citizens to be executed with these means without a formal process of appeal, to the emperor directly if necessary. That would have tied the proceedings up for years, and the sort of large-scale executions as described by historians would not have possibly been carried out in such a short time (Lampe 2003: 82).

That followers of Jesus in Rome were mainly resident aliens should come as no surprise. Other than slaves and a small percentage of citizens, the vast majority of those living in early imperial Rome were aliens. They were immigrants, freedmen and freedwomen, manumitted former slaves brought in from the provinces, and freeborn to non-citizen parents. In principle, slaves could be granted citizenship upon manumission, but only at the discretion of their masters (Balsdon 1979: 86). Presumably this was how some of the urban Jews received their citizenship (Lampe 2003: 83–4). The passage of the *lex Iunia Norbana* of 19 CE put a stop to granting citizenship automatically to manumitted slaves, however. Manumitted slaves could become freedmen and freedwomen while alive but they would revert to their slave status upon death – to allow their former masters to claim their estate (Balsdon 1979: 87; Hassall 1987: 694). This new law vastly limited the slaves' path to citizenship and contributed to the swelling ranks of foreigners in the capital. Resident aliens and their children could become citizens after twenty-five years of service in the auxiliary regiments, but even after acquiring citizenship, their former social status stayed with them throughout their lives. From archaeological evidence, it is made clear that aliens made up three-quarters of Rome's population in the first century (Brunt 1971: 102; Balsdon 1979: 13–14). Resentment of their presence fuelled xenophobia, as can be seen through the scathing barbs by elites like Seneca (*De consolatione ad Helvium* 11.6.2–3) and the satirist Juvenal (*Satires* 3 & 6).

All foreigners experienced a common pattern. In Rome, they were regarded socially as outsiders and legally as perpetual migrants, even if their family had lived there for generations. Extra tax burdens were levied on non-citizens. They were subject to an annual poll or tribute tax (*tributum capitis*) and a land tax (*tributum soli*), from which Roman citizens were exempt (Burton 1987: 427). Paul raises the issue of taxation in Rom. 13.6–7, likely because members of the Roman congregation were levied the tribute taxes (*phoroi*). As for their legal rights and protection, resident aliens and their children were granted the basic rights to which all human beings were entitled (*ius gentium*) but little else. They were deprived of the right to vote (*ius suffragiorum*). They were not allowed to serve in the legions, which was a sure way of climbing the social ladder and earning citizenship, only in the less prestigious auxiliary regiments. They were denied the right to hold property (*ius commercii*) and the right to intermarry with citizens (*ius connubii*). Children born under a mixed union between a non-citizen and a citizen were considered illegitimate and were not allowed to inherit citizenship or property from their parents. Unless they had served in the regiments, resident aliens were not allowed to designate an heir to their possessions. Migrants who lived in an urban centre like Rome lost not only their physical homeland; in time, after several generations and a long process of assimilation, they lost even the conception of a homeland when there was no prospect of return and the promise of Roman citizenship was deferred to an illusive future. These foreigners formed the core of the audience at whom Paul aimed his missive.

Paul's intended audience was also likely drawn from the lower classes in Roman society, which would be consistent with the immigration status of the majority of its members. According to Robert Jewett, four of the five groups in Romans 16 are mentioned without a patron. The expression 'those who belong to the Aristoboulos' found in 16.10 suggests that the patron himself was not a follower of Christ but his clients under his employ were. Likewise 'those who are of Narkissos' are 'in the Lord' (16.11) but the patron himself was not. These groups would be meeting in their own living quarters but they would not be supervised by someone with high status. The two groups mentioned in 16.14 and 16.15 are full of Greek names of slaves, so no one would be the patron. Those named were likely charismatic leaders in charge of the meeting cells. All this leads Jewett to conclude that the persons named were of low status. They would be meeting not in villas or large halls under the patronage of a well-to-do patriarch but rather in tenements (*insulae*) without the benefit of a patronage. The social arrangement of these groups was nonpatriarchal in that leaders exercised leadership by ability and charisma and not by dint of their social station. They practiced a form of 'agapaic communalism' according to which all who belong to the cell shared their possessions in common and supported each other with meals in the context of sacramental celebrations (Jewett 2006: 65–7, 966–7, 969–72; also Jewett 1993).

The Congregation through Paul's Eyes

At the time Paul composed his missive to the Roman congregation, its exiled Jewish leaders must have been allowed to return to Rome, perhaps for some time already. Erstwhile leaders Priska and Aquila had re-established a congregation in their house, to whom Paul sends his greetings (Rom. 16.3–5). That the two were able to own properties in Corinth (Acts 18.2), Ephesus (1 Cor. 16.19), and Rome (Rom. 16.5) large enough to house congregations and that they had the means to travel bespeak their high social status (Jewett 2006: 958). This is confirmed by Paul's effusive praise heaped upon them, calling them his 'fellow workers in Christ Jesus' who 'risked their necks for my life, to whom not only I but all the assemblies of the Gentiles give thanks' (Rom. 16.3–4). By calling them 'fellow workers', Paul introduces them to his Roman audience as fellow missionaries equal to him in prestige, and with the expression 'risked their necks', Paul makes known that they had saved his life at considerable risk to their own. Both facts would fit in well with the likely suggestion that they were Paul's patrons. What is odd, however, is that Paul insists that 'all the assemblies of the Gentiles' owe the two Jewish leaders their gratitude. While active in the Pauline mission, Priska and Aquila could not have done work that could be said to have benefited 'all' Gentile congregations. Paul could have made such a wild exaggeration only for a calculated reason: to lend his apostolic name to the re-acceptance of the couple in their former circles.[9] The absence of former Jewish leaders had made it possible for the Gentiles to seize control of the Roman congregations, but the return of leaders like Priska and Aquila was now the occasion for intense negotiation between the two groups vying for control (Wiefel 1991).

Paul was aware of the dispute between Jews and Gentiles, but textual evidence suggests that he had made the strategic move of writing only to the Gentiles. Three times Paul explicitly addresses his audience in Romans, and each time, he calls them 'Gentiles' (Stowers 1994: 29–36; Elliott 2008: 19 & 177 n. 67; Lampe 2003: 70 & n. 3), and concomitantly he reminds his readers time and again that he is called to be 'an apostle to the Gentiles'. In his self-introduction he presents the aim of his mission as bringing about 'an obedience of faith among all the Gentiles, among whom you yourselves are called to be Jesus Christ's' (1.5–6), stressing to his audience his status as apostle and their subordination or obedience to him. He returns to the expression towards the end of Romans (15.18–19) to re-assert his superiority. In his construction of his relation to his audience, he assumes the role of a superior teacher of Jewish wisdom and excavator of the holy scriptures. In the thanksgiving prayer, Paul informs his audience that even though he is visiting Rome for the first time, he does so as an apostle whose job it is 'to reap some fruit among you', where 'you' is constructed explicitly as Gentiles, and 'Gentiles' are understood to be comprised of 'Greeks and barbarians' (1.13–14). In spite of his unfamiliarity with the audience, he co-opts them under his charge. Finally, in his climactic argument for the future salvation of 'all Israel' (11.25–27), he speaks from his elevated perch as apostle: 'I speak to you Gentiles – inasmuch as I myself an apostle to the Gentiles and

---

[9] Jewett (2006: 958) notes the strategic value of Paul's exaggeration but takes it into a rather unlikely abstract direction.

I glorify my ministry... ' (11.13). With the elaborate allegory of the olive tree symbolizing the Jewish covenant (11.17–24), Paul stresses to his Gentile audience that they have been granted entry into a *Jewish* covenant. Gentiles should have no part of it if not for an extraordinary act of divine grace. They are but 'wild olive branches' grafted in place of the original, domesticated branches momentarily lobbed off, so they could share in the roots' rich sap (11.17). Then comes a warning intended to put the Gentiles in their place: 'Do not boast at the expense of the [original] branches. If you boast, [know that] you do not support the root but the root you' (11.18).

It has puzzled generations of interpreters why Paul would want 'to bear some fruit among you..., to evangelize even those... in Rome' (1.13, 15), when that seems to violate his stated principle of not treading on others' turf (Rom. 15.20; cf. also 2 Cor. 10.13, 15). The Roman congregation already existed before Paul's proposed visit (Rom. 1.11; 15.22–23). To evangelize an already-established congregation would also be most impolitic if Paul hopes to win support for his Spanish mission. The problem disappears if this is understood as part of Paul's pattern of establishing himself as the rabbinic authority over against Gentile novices. 'To evangelize' here means not so much making new converts or founding new congregation as in the political-theological sense of announcing the advent of a new king, the messianic Son of God foretold by the prophets. In that case Paul is gesturing towards to a celebration with his recipients of Christ's universal kingship over against a Roman propaganda that touts the emperor's supposed godlike status. In 15.20 Paul uses 'to evangelize' in the sense of proclaiming the good news to Gentiles, who have never heard of Jesus: 'Thus I aspire to evangelize not where Christ has already been names, in order not to build on someone else's foundation, but as it is written, "Those to whom it has not been proclaimed of him will see, and those who have not heard will understand" (Isa. 52.15)'. Given the weight the verb carried within the Jesus-movement and usage elsewhere, Paul's use of it in the introduction is integral to his concerted effort of assuming the role of a superior rabbi in relation to his Gentile audience. What is encoded in the use of evangelization vocabulary, in other words, is an assertion of power over his Gentile audience.

In Rom. 2.17, Paul appears to be addressing Jews, but he probably has in mind Gentile converts who wish to push the Jesus-movement towards stricter observance of Torah. The context gives it away. Whether circumcision is necessary for an authentic Jewish identity (2.25–29) is the question that occasioned a crisis in Galatia. There the question was whether Gentile followers should circumcise before they are accepted as full members of the covenant. Then as now, Paul's answer is a resounding No (Gal. 5.2). But circumcision is an issue that concerns only adult Gentile converts; for Jews it is a standard part of one's upbringing that occasions no controversy. When it has to do with circumcision for Jews, Paul uses it matter-of-factly as a synecdoche for Jews (Gal. 2.7, 8, 9; Phil. 3.3). It is stated as an unspoken assumption that needs no explication, because he expects every Jewish male to have, as he has, been circumcised as a newborn on the eighth day (Phil. 3.5).

That is why Paul addresses his Gentile reader not as 'you Jew' but as 'you *who call yourself a* Jew' (Rom. 2.17). Converts to Judaism would identify themselves as 'Jews', and that would apply to converts who also happen to be followers of Jesus. That is how Paul addresses the Thessalonian converts who 'turned to God from idols to serve a living and true God' (1 Thess. 1.9). After their conversion, Paul assumes their Jewishness and instructs them not to give in to impurity or passions 'like the *Gentiles* who do not know God' (1 Thess. 4.5; Eisenbaum 2009: 157–8).

Paul's language and substance are reminiscent of the Stoic philosopher Epictetus's response to those who play-act the part of a philosopher without a corresponding change of one's inner life:

> Why then do you *call yourself* a Stoic? Why do you mislead the common folk? Why do you play-act a Jew even though you are Greek? Don't you see how each is called a Jew, a Syrian, an Egyptian? Whenever we see someone equivocating, we are wont to say, 'He is not a Jew but is only acting'. But when he adopts the inner sentiments of one who has been baptized (*baptizesthai*) and made his choice, then he is both in fact and is called a Jew. Likewise we are also falsely baptized (*parabaptistai*), in name Jews but in reality something else, if we are unsympathetic to our own reason, far from practicing what we say, haughty as if we knew them.
>
> (Epictetus, *Diss.* 2.9.19–21)

Epictetus probably mistook Gentile followers of Jesus for regular converts to Judaism. Jews practiced the rite of ablution, but baptism was what Christianity was known for and what distinguished it from all other philosophies (Wan 2009: 149–51). Paul's argument in Romans is similar. Because these converts are unsympathetic to their inner sentiments, they are only play-acting (literally 'hypocritizing') Jews in word or in deed (Wan 2009).

Modern readers conditioned by centuries of mischaracterization of Judaism as legalistic might point to 2.1–16 as evidence of Paul addressing

Jews. That would be unlikely. Paul takes up these accoutrements of Judaism in this section in order to assume the role of a superior rabbi lecturing his Gentile students. Paul's derisive reminder to his audience that 'they are instructed in the law' (2.18) gives it away. The verb literally means 'to catechize' and was later used in the specific sense of instructing new converts to Christianity's basic tenets of the faith (Luke 1.4; Acts 18.25; 21.21, 24; *2 Clement* 17.1). But the word might well have acquired a similar meaning already by Paul's time. When Paul uses it twice in Gal. 6.6, he has in mind the instruction of converts (Jewett 2006: 224), as he does in 1 Cor. 14.19. Besides, hypocrisy was not a Jewish monopoly, and there is little evidence that only Judaism was attacked for it.

It is far more likely that Paul here uses a common argumentative style called diatribe, through which one raises a hypothetical question by an imaginary or real interlocutor for elaboration or dismissal (Elliott 1990; Stowers 1994: 122–33). When Paul exclaims, 'Therefore you have no excuse, O man or woman, everyone of you who judges' (2.1), he directs his criticism not to Judaism but to the generic arrogant persons whose discrepancy between what they say and what they do opens themselves to the charge of hypocrisy. So, Paul asks, 'Do you who teach another teach yourself? Do you who preach against stealing steal? Does he who forbids adultery commit adultery? Does he who detests idols rob temples? Do you who boast in the law dishonor God through transgression against the law?' (2.21–23). The more likely scenario is, when Paul taunts 'If you call yourself a Jew' (2.17), he is addressing Gentiles who regard themselves as full converts to Judaism but whose supercilious adherence to the commandments, in particular circumcision, makes them hyper-judgemental of others who do not share their views.[10] When the Claudian expulsion decimated Jewish leadership in the burgeoning assemblies, these converts took up the mantle of leadership but, in their overzealousness, also imposed strict rules on following the commandments.

To respond to the situation, Paul reminds them of their Gentile identity and constructs a hierarchy based on ethnicity. In expressing his intention to reap some fruit 'among you as among the rest of the Gentiles; both to Greeks and to barbarians, both to the wise and to the foolish I am a debtor' (1.13–14), he links up 'Greeks and Barbarians' to 'Gentiles', in order to equate the two. The pejorative term 'barbarians' was first devised by the Greeks to

---

[10] Paul's use of 'Gentiles' in Rom. 2.24, 'The name of God is blasphemed among the Gentiles because of you' (citing Isa. 52.5), should probably be understood in the same way as it is used in 1 Thess. 4.5.

distinguish themselves from those they regarded as their cultural inferior.[11] It was part of a complex formula constructed to exclude the ethnic 'other' (Hall 1997) that the Romans adapted to their advantage. In using a phrase familiar to his audience, Paul signals a willingness to accede to their ethnic categories. But he does so only to submerge it under his own division of humanity – 'to the Jew first, then to the Greek', a phrase he repeats four times in the opening section of the letter (1.16; 2.9, 10; 3.9; see also 10.12). In so doing Paul makes his priority clear: His Roman audience might see themselves as superior to the barbarian other, but in Paul's construction Greeks and barbarians are both Gentiles in contradistinction from the Jews. That hierarchy is expressed most clearly in the allegory of the olive tree.

Paul's division into Jews and Gentiles is structurally similar to his Roman audience's division between Greeks and barbarians in that both are based on a form of universalism (Wan 2009: 139–41). But in substituting Greco-Roman universalism with Jewish universalism, Paul codeswitches to a construction that allows him to tap into a set of rights and obligations the new language affords him (Myers-Scotton 1993). So when Paul folds his audience's ethnic categories into his own, he redoubles his construction of his audience as Gentiles to co-opt them into his preferred ethnic categories. In codeswitching, Paul constructs a rhetorical strategy that compels his audience to take the vantage point of Gentiles and to look up to Paul as the expert Jewish pedagogue, an apostle to the Gentiles. In using 'Jew and Greek' to describe humanity, Paul therefore appeals to two ethnic myths simultaneously. All 'Jews' are now made to stand together in an ethnic myth of sameness. They are set opposite to the 'Greeks', who are now made to stand for all non-Jews, who are flattened into a sameness, regardless of their actual ethnicity, for no other reason than they are different from insiders, the 'Jews'.[12]

---

[11] So Aristotle: 'Therefore say the poets, "It is fitting that Greeks should govern barbarians", since barbarian and slave are in nature the same' (Aristotle, *Politics* 1.1252b8–9).

[12] Some have argued that because no people in the ancient world would call themselves 'Gentiles' but only 'Greeks', 'Persians', 'Parthians', and so on, Paul could not be using 'Greeks' to refer to all Gentiles (Stanley 1996: 101–24; Sumney 2007: 59; Elliott 2008: 46). But here Paul is not engaged in a sociological exercise but an ideological construct for the sake of rhetorical persuasion. He is using the language of insiders – as defined by old boundaries based on bloodline, lineage, and genealogy. Only a Jew would find it acceptable to divide humanity into 'Jews and Greeks'. Only a Greek or, by proxy, a Roman would accept the division of the world into 'Greeks and barbarians'. All these statements are self-evidently ethnocentric in that they privilege one ethnic group by using in-group language as standards to evaluate outsiders. What Paul adopts here is what anthropologists call an *emic* (in-group, idiosyncratic) perspective from which to evaluate the world in terms consistent with his Jewish identity and tradition, as opposed to an *etic* approach, which uses out-group, scientific, analytic language to describe an 'objective' reality and to allow for comparison of different groups.

Purpose of Romans

It is time to draw some conclusions on why Paul expends so much time and resource developing an elaborate opus like Romans. At first glance, it seems easy to rely on what he expressly tells his audience towards the conclusion of the letter, that he wants to visit Rome on his way to Spain, 'for I hope to see you on my way and *to be sent (propempein)* there by you after I first fully enjoy your company for a while' (15.23–24; see also v. 28). *Propempein* means 'to assist in a journey by providing personnel, money, food, and other means of travel' (BDAG 2000: 873; Acts 20.38; 21.5; 1 Cor. 16.11; 2 Cor. 1.16). Within the Jesus-movement, the word acquires a semi-technical meaning of provisioning for a missionary journey (Acts 15.3; 1 Cor. 16.6; Tit. 3.13; 3 Jn 6), and that is Paul's usage here as well. With no further place in the Aegean regions to carry out his mission, he says, he now writes the Roman congregation with the hope that they would support him with financial and material means necessary for a mission to Spain.

Why Spain? In Roman cartography and biblical symbolism, Spain was the proverbial 'ends of the earth' (so Acts 1.8). Judging from his travel plans disclosed in Romans, Paul probably thought of it as the final destination in his Gentile mission. Spain stands at the western end on ancient maps of the Mediterranean world (the Peutinger Map, which is a copy of an originally first-century map) and holds a mystique as the terminus of travel westward. In the context of Paul's own apocalyptic vision, he probably interpreted the Isaianic vision of gathering all nations to Zion (Isaiah 66) as being fulfilled by his Gentile mission to Spain (Munck 1959; Aus 1979). Tarshish of Isa. 66.19 has been identified as the Spanish harbour city of Tartessos on the coast of the Iberian Peninsula, just beyond the Pillars of Hercules, modern-day Strait of Gibraltar. The Greeks thought European civilization originated from Tartessos, while biblical tradition identifies Tarshish as the ends of the earth (e.g., LXX Ps. 71.8, 10; Jon. 1.3; Jewett 2006: 924 & n 32).[13]

If Paul hopes to win support from the Roman congregation for his proposed mission, he is faced with an immediate hurdle. Unlike congregations he founded, such as those in Galatia, Philippi, Thessalonica, and Corinth, congregations indebted to him, he has no personal connection to Rome and holds little sway over it. He admits that he is visiting the

---

[13] Aus (1979: 244) suggests that Ps. Sol. 8.16 (15) depicts Pompey coming from Spain, the 'ends of the earth'.

capital for the first time (15.22), reiterating what is said in the thanksgiving prayer (1.10, 13), thereby conceding the weakness of his position. There is another, even more daunting obstacle, which has to do with his reputation. The extensive list of names dropped in Romans 16, a separate letter of recommendation for Phoebe (16.1), tells us that Paul is not an unknown to the Roman congregation. There is enough traffic between the capital and the rest of the empire for the Roman congregation to know Paul, by reputation if not in person. Nevertheless, the Romans owe Paul no allegiance. In fact, his controversial positions on circumcision and his public clash with Peter and James (Gal. 2.11–14) might well have made Paul a liability to any congregation entertaining the thought of supporting him.

Because of his reputation, he now finds it necessary to strike a balance between on the one hand asserting his apostolic authority, which may or may not have currency in an unfamiliar congregation, and on the other winning the trust of his audience and their support for his mission. This delicate negotiation between apostolic entitlement and humility is evident in the thanksgiving prayer. Paul starts by erecting a lofty perch from which to address his audience: 'For I desire to see you to impart to you certain spiritual gift in order that you be strengthened' (Rom. 1.11). The verb 'to impart', not 'to share' (NRSV), befits someone of high status providing for someone of a lower status. That would be Paul's natural position to take (see, e.g., 1 Thess. 2.8). But he seems to understand how unproductive that position is, for he immediately softens his tone by suggesting that the Romans 'be strengthened'. Paul deliberately uses a passive verb to disconnect himself from the gift, while also hinting at divine agency. To reinforce the point, Paul adds a grace note: 'that is, to be mutually encouraged among you through the faith in each other – both yours and mine' (1.12). This show of humility is more apparent than real, however: 'To be mutually encouraged' parallels 'be strengthened', and both are predicated on Paul's imparting his spiritual gift to his would-be hosts.

In light of the proposed Spanish mission and his own reputation, then, Paul wrote this letter in part to correct possible misconceptions of his positions and in part to provide an extended self-introduction to a congregation unfamiliar with him. Romans, in other words, is a letter of recommendation for himself complete with a coherent presentation of his vision of the gospel. Such a theory would explain the relatively orderly nature of his presentation. It would also help explain why Paul reworks topics first broached elsewhere, such as circumcision, Abraham, the Last Adam, the body of Christ, the strong and the weak, and so on. At the same time, to gain Roman support for his mission, Paul must make a case for the essential correctness of his message, as he was compelled at the Jerusalem meeting to lay before '[the acknowledged leaders] the gospel I preached among the Gentiles ..., lest somehow I was running or had run in vain' (Gal. 2.2). The assumption, then as now, is that Paul's gospel to the Gentiles had a recognizable shape and could be tested. The standards of correctness, however, were not found in observable rules but rested with the Jerusalem leadership. There is no evidence that the Jerusalem leadership had jurisdiction over the congregation in Rome. But given Paul's eagerness to inform his Roman audience of his impending trip to Jerusalem to deliver the collection for the poor (Rom. 15.25–27) – he goes out of his way to make mention of that trip – Rome was probably on friendly terms with Jerusalem.

What underlies Paul's mission is an apocalyptic event, the resurrection of Jesus of Nazareth that installs him as the cosmic Son of God. The resurrection signals to Paul that the long-awaited reign of God is about to break into history and that the Davidic kingship will be restored, resulting in the founding of an ideal Israel based on the justice of God. Paul's message in Romans is political-theological, and his 'task at hand is the *establishment and legitimation of a new people of God*' (Taubes 2004: 28; emphasis original). Such a vision could not have escaped the charge of subversion by an empire that regarded conquest and expansion of territories as its birthright and divine entitlements – if only the imperial censors knew what they were reading or hearing. What sets Paul apart from his fellow Jewish contemporaries, though, is his insistence that Gentiles be part of Ideal Israel. His categorization of humanity into Jews and Gentiles lays an intellectual foundation for the people of God, but it also issues a challenge to the imperial division into Romans and barbarians. Just as the Roman slogan is a claim to universal rulership, that the world be organized in reference to the centre, Paul's counter-assertion claims equal universality. The key to Roman ethnography was to bifurcate the world into 'enlightened rulers' who must rule and savages who must be 'pacified' and civilized. The Roman mandate to expand its empire was predicated on naming other races and peoples as inferior, without whom Roman superiority could not have existed. The Empire could not have been the mighty empire that it was without the barbarians. Paul follows a similar script. Without the Gentiles the Jewish messiah would be little more than a local chieftain and his preaching could never hope to rival the 'good news' of the mighty Romans. But the inclusion of Gentiles transforms a local Jewish phenomenon into a universal claim over the inhabited world. This is the reason for Paul's urgency to preach the good news in Rome (1.15) but more importantly to Spain, the biblical ends of the earth (15.24, 28). The inclusion of Gentiles in Ideal Israel is what enables Paul to transform a Jewish king into a cosmic Son of God, and that turns out to be a critical step in the development of Paul's political-theological thinking, When Paul is engaged in the construction of Ideal Israel, he is working towards a reign that directly challenges the Empire, and Gentiles play an indispensable role by being incorporated into a new peoplehood. Ethnic issues are not tangential to the purpose of Romans but central to it. In foregrounding them, Paul is not innocent of imperializing ambitions. He learned his lessoned from his imperial master too well.

Paul's vision also involves the formation of a New Community capable of challenging the Empire from within. If the evangel is all about the arrival of a new king, then 'to evangelize' implies a need for the formation of a New Community. Paul never clarifies how the New Community might take part in the reconstruction of Ideal Israel. In fact, he takes great care to insure no one mistakes the New Community for Ideal Israel. But his attention to the characters and ethics of this community, especially in chapters 12–15, suggests that he freights it with high hope and regards it as a critical first step towards Ideal Israel. Paul reminds his Gentile audience they are included because of mercy, but he is equally adamant that they will never supplant the original occupants of the covenant in his olive tree allegory (11.17–24). He explicitly and condescendingly calls them 'You Gentiles!' (11.13) before sternly warning them not to boast, because 'it is not you who bears the root but the root you' (11.18). He also terms the eventual salvation of 'all Israel' a 'mystery,' thus relegating it to the realm of divine revelation and, more importantly, disconnecting the restoration of Ideal Israel from the New Community (11.25–26).

We must therefore take great care not to mistake the New Community for Ideal Israel. Paul is not proposing in Romans what the second-century church called a 'third race', Christians to be distinguished from both Jews and Gentiles. Paul is clear that the new people are based on God's original covenant with Israel. His genius is to convince the Gentiles that through an extraordinary show of grace, God has extended an invitation to them, former enemies, to be part of this covenant. The final aim is not so much to create a new people replacing an old as to renew an ancient people by pushing its ethnic boundaries outwards until they encompass all nations and all ethnicities, crossing and erasing old boundaries. Paul's resolution of the conflicts between Jews and Gentiles does not replace his anti-imperial criticism but embodies it.[14] The inclusion of Gentiles into the covenant is the very instrument by which the new peoplehood is realized.

Paul's thesis statement – 'For I am not ashamed of the gospel, for it is the power of God for the salvation of everyone who has faith, to the Jew first then the Greek, for the justice of God is revealed from faith to faith, as it is written, "The just out of faith will live"' (1.16–17) – names four interlocking themes to be fleshed out in the rest of Romans. First, he makes a case for including the Gentiles in Ideal Israel by incorporating them as legitimate descendants of Abraham (1.18–4.25). Second, the justice of God, contrary to Roman justice, is established not by human decree but by divine revelation, and not as a pretext for conquest but for the purpose of renewing a creation subject to decay and corruption (5.1–8.39). Third, salvation of all Israel is guaranteed by God's faithfulness and will be reaffirmed in the end time (9.1–11.36). Before the end time, fourth, members of the New Community must conduct themselves worthy of their identity and their calling (12.1–15.13). What unifies all four themes is God's faithfulness and the call for our obedience to what God is doing. These four themes will be explored in the following chapter.

---

[14] Neil Elliott voices a similar concern: 'Paul's apostolic work was in inevitable conflict with the Augustan vision of the obedience of nations. We miss that tension if we persist in reading Romans on strictly ethnic terms, as Paul's effort to smooth tension arising between ethnic groups, Jews… and Gentiles, and to promote a tolerant universalism between these groups' (Elliott 2008: 47).

2

Reading Romans

Ideal Israel (Romans 1–4)

In the opening section, Paul seeks to demonstrate that Gentiles are legitimate descendants of Abraham, but he must do so in the context of a contentious relationship between overzealous Gentiles and former Jewish leaders now returning to Rome. He advices the Gentiles not to become so focused on the external trappings of their conversion to Judaism that they lose sight of fulfilling the law. As legitimate descendants of Abraham, they must become what their identity says they are and practice what the law says. Inclusion of Gentiles in the Abrahamic covenant raises a serious problem, however. If former Gentiles could be considered legitimate heir of the Abrahamic promise, what advantage does Judaism have and what makes it unique? The Jesus-movement is becoming more and more Gentile while fewer and fewer Jews join the movement. Can the movement retain any credibility if the original members of the covenant are left out of it? Paul teases with this question until it is answered in full later in chapters 9–11.

A Rhetorical Trap (1.18–32)

The body of Romans is often thought to begin with Paul's matching criticisms against Gentile impiety (1.18–32) and Jewish hypocrisy (2.1–29), thereby establishing a universal plight to which Christ is offered as solution. There are three problems with such a reading. First, it would reduce the political and ethnic tensions in the letter opening to timeless doctrines.

Second, there is little evidence that Paul makes negative statements against Jews or Judaism in his letter to the Romans. In fact, the opposite is true. He defends the superiority of the Jews, who 'have been entrusted with God's oracles' (3.2) and calls them affectionately 'my kinsfolk' (9.3). He upholds the vitality and continual validity of the Mosaic Law (3.31), calling it 'holy' and its commandments 'holy, just, and good' (7.12). He touts the uniqueness of Abraham and his genealogy (4.1–3). Most important, he takes great pride in the special prerogatives available only to Jews (9.4–5) and insists that in spite of their momentary lapse, God is faithful and will not abandon the elect (11.1, 26). All this makes it doubtful that Paul here rejects his fellow-Jews or his beloved Judaism. Third, if the disquisition on idol worship and immorality were meant a lengthy condemnation of Gentiles in the abstract, it misses the mark by a wide margin. As discussed in Chapter 1, the intended recipients are *converts* who have taken over leadership of the congregation from their absent Jewish colleagues. They would have 'turned to God from idols to serve a living and true God' (1 Thess. 1.9–10) and would be the opposite of those who 'did not glorify or give thanks to God as God…, but exchanged the glory of the incorruptible God for images in the likeness of a corruptible human being and fowls and quadrupeds and reptiles' (Rom. 1.21, 23). They would have regarded themselves as 'Jews' even if Paul insists on constructing them still as 'Gentiles'.

The key to reading this passage is to recognize how stereotypical and unremarkable it is. Gentiles are accused for their unwillingness to discern the creator through the created order and their worship of creatures and human beings instead of the creator (1.19–23). The Gentiles' propensity for idol worship was a standard trope among Greek-speaking Jewish writers. The author of the *Wisdom of Solomon* characterizes Gentiles this way: 'On account of the visible good things they were powerless to know the Being, nor did they recognize the artisan while paying heed to his works… Again they are not excused, for if they had the power to know so much that they could investigate the world, how did they fail to find the Lord of these things sooner?' (Wis. 13.1–2, 8–9 NRSV adapted). Refusing to acknowledge God's creatorship, Gentiles turn to 'dead things' and 'call works by human hands "gods"' (Wis. 13.10). An anonymous sermon from a Greek-speaking synagogue makes a similar point (Pseudo-Philonic *De Jona* 4.10–5.19; 31.121–34.134, especially 33.125–129). Greco-Roman philosophers like Epictetus, Seneca, and Cicero also agreed that God's design could be inferred from creation, and the refusal to acknowledge the manifestly obvious only makes one stupid and dim. Those who would hold such opinions were inexcusable (Keener 2009: 32–34). Gentiles were held accountable for not honouring the creator despite the possibility for knowledge. Ignorance was no excuse.

As with his contemporaries, Paul attributes Gentile immorality to the consequence of not knowing the creator: '*Therefore*, God delivered them up in the passions of their hearts for impurity, in order that their bodies might be dishonored among themselves' (Rom. 1.24; also v. 26). As illustrations of 'dishonorable passions', he follows convention and lists same-sex relation (1.26–27). Criticism of same-sex relation was also part of a standard trope. Philo, for example, rejected it on the ground that it was 'against nature', a term Paul also embraces. To be 'natural', however, demanded that the dominant male penetrate the subordinate female (Philo, *De Abrahamo* 135–37; also Josephus, *Contra Apionum* 2.199, 215). The catalogue of vices in 1.29–31 can similarly be found among Hellenistic philosophers, who used it to eliminate character defects through self-control.

The appeal to cultural norms is in fact part of Paul's argument. He does not set out to prove that same-sex relation is wrong; he begins with that premise and uses it 'to prove' the deleterious effects of idolatry on morality – hence the use of 'therefore' in an emphatic position. He uses same-sex relation and other vices to make his point precisely because they are part of the unexamined cultural biases he expects his audience to hold. These statements are not so much timeless doctrines as they are ethnographic observations.

Doers of the Law (2.1–29)

There is only one reason why Paul resorts to standard tropes he knows his audience would agree with, and that is to reel them in before charging them with hypocrisy. These familiar vices set up a rhetorical trap to spring on those who think Paul is repeating their talking points until he uses their biases against them. The abrupt change in tone is a dead giveaway: '*Therefore* you have no excuse, O man or woman, you who pass judgement, for you condemn yourself in the very thing that you judge the other, for you who judge practice the very same things' (2.1). 'Therefore' sets this section up as a consequence of what comes before. 'O man or woman!' ('whoever you are' NRSV) is a standard feature in a common pedagogical style called diatribe that was used primarily in a classroom setting. The teacher would use imaginary interlocutors to lead students to a recognition of their errors and a deeper understanding of the subject matter (Stowers 1994; Longenecker 2016: 244). Such a posture would fit well with how Paul introduces himself as an experienced rabbi giving instructions to Gentile converts.

A number of verbal clues link this section to the last. Those who judge others 'have no excuse' (2.1), just as those who fail to discern the creator from creation also 'have no excuse' (1.20). Both 'practice' the same thing that could merit death (1.32) or judgement (2.1–3). This stress on practice allows Paul to establish that a true Jew is one who not just hears the Torah but does what it says (2.13). He first asserts that judgement on the last day is based on one's deeds (2.5–6) and that the present lull is the result of God's forbearance and must not be taken as acceptance of evil deeds (2.4).

Protestant interpreters conditioned by centuries of denigrating good work might be surprised by the classic two-way theology in 2.7–10, but Paul does so to highlight the phrase 'to the Jew first then to the Greek', mentioned twice in these verses. The phrase shows, first of all, when meting out punishment and reward, 'God shows no partiality' (2.11). Both Jews and Gentiles, which is Paul's way of saying the totality of all humanity, are judged on the same basis – that is, by their work. But why emphasize the priority of the Jews over the Gentiles? It is aimed at the overzealous Gentile converts eager to replace the former Jewish leaders. When introduced in 1.16, the phrase 'to the Jew first then to the Greek' reminded Gentile converts of the Jewish priority in offering the gospel. The intent here is similar: It is through the Jews that standards for divine judgement are established for all humanity, in particular those who measure themselves against Jews. Gentiles who 'call themselves Jews' (3.17) are judged by the same criterion, which always has to do what the law says. Inasmuch as Gentiles have knowledge of the creator (1.19–20), they are a law unto themselves if they do what is written in their hearts (2.14–15). Here Paul applies Jeremiah's new covenant to Gentiles: God puts the law in their hearts so that 'they shall all know me, from the least of them to the greatest' (Jer. 31.33–34; cf. also Ezek. 36.26–27). That implies the written code has lost its unique character, because all who do what is in their hearts are now counted as righteous (Rom. 2.13).

That the intended target is the Gentile converts is confirmed when Paul reminds them they have been 'catechized' (*katēchousthai*) in the law (2.18). They boast of their new standing in the congregation, their instruction in the law, and their role as teachers to others (2.19–23). For them circumcision has become a badge of honour (2.24–29), proof of their credential. Paul responds by stressing that only 'doers of the law', not 'hearers of the law', are justified (2.13). 'Doer' and 'hearer' are here used as labels, because they define one's inner character. The only standard that counts is not whether one is circumcised but whether one is a habitual doer of the law. So, 'circumcision is of use if you practice the law' (2.25), and a 'transgressor of the law' (2.25, 27) – that is, one who is characterized by habitual transgression – turns one's circumcision into uncircumcision, whereas an uncircumcision (not just the uncircumcised) that keeps the law is counted as circumcision (2.25–27).

These themes are all gathered up in a climactic statement with a subtle nod to Jeremiah: 'For he who is [a Jew] in the open is not a Jew, nor is the [circumcision] in the open, on the flesh, circumcision; rather, he who is hidden [is] a Jew, and a circumcision of the heart, in spirit and not letter, [is circumcision]' (2.28–29). Taken out of context, these lines can be mistaken for a denigration of physical Judaism. In the context of Romans, however, Paul uses them to correct overzealous converts by pointing out what the physical rite signifies: 'circumcision is of use if you practice the law' (2.25). He chides them for elevating the physical rite at the expense of fulfilling its requirements. In comparison to his words to the Galatians (Gal. 5.2), Paul's view here is surprisingly positive: 'circumcision of the heart in spirit' opens up a path for a constructive appropriation, a path that was indeed taken by a later disciple (Col. 2.11–13).

Inclusion of Gentiles (3.1–31)

That Paul does not dismiss physical Judaism is clear from his vigorous defence of the Jews and the law in Rom. 3.1–8. He does so in typical diatribe style – by posing rhetorical questions. He fires off four in rapid succession. The first is triggered by his earlier statement that Gentiles could be 'a law unto themselves' (2.14). If that is the case, what privilege do the Jews have and what is so special about circumcision? (3.1). His answer: 'first and foremost they have been entrusted with the oracles of God' (3.2). The second question has to do with why at present his fellow-Jews are shunning the Jesus-movement: 'If some did not have faith (*apistein*), their lack of faith (*apistia*) does not nullify the faithfulness (*pistis*) of God, does it?' (3.3). Relying on a play on words based on the *pist*-root, Paul answers in the negative: God is faithful and human beings are liars (3.4). That brings up a third question:

'If our injustice (*adikia*) establishes God's justice (*dikaiosynē*), God is not unjust (*adikos*) [to punish us], is he?' (3.5). This time playing on words of the *dik*-root, he likewise answers, 'No!' (3.6–7). The fourth question answers critics who mischaracterize his position as advocating evil to increase good, to whom he pronounces 'condemnation!' (3.8). These questions, in particular the first three, all have to do with Paul's Jewish kinsfolk, or Physical Israel, to whom Paul will return in chapters 9–11. For now they open up a consideration of Ideal Israel (3.9–4.25), which is characterized by God's justice and faithfulness (chapters 5–8).

His statement on Ideal Israel (3.9–20) begins with a statement on universal culpability, 'both Jews and Greeks are all under sin' (3.9), but there is a crucial change in perspective. This statement is an answer to the question, 'What then, do *we* have an advantage?'[1] In codeswitching to 'we', Paul signals to his Gentile audience that they are now entering a discursive space on Judaism in which he, the superior rabbi, alone has the authority to propound. He declares that his own kinsfolk, Jews entrusted with the oracles, are no better off: reception of the law does not guarantee blamelessness unless it is put into practice. On the contrary, possession of the oracles raises culpability, a point he proves by scriptural texts (3.10–18). Paul then concludes, '*We* know that whatever the law says it speaks to those in the law…, because out of the works of the law no flesh will be justified in his presence…' (3.19–20). To Jews a message of universal culpability is hardly earth shattering; self-criticism is standard fare in the Prophets. To Gentiles who yearn to be accepted into Judaism, however, to share the same discursive space and achieve parity with Jews – in transgression and in redemption – would be a liberating development. They are now members of the same people with Jews in need of atonement. In including them in the general condition of universal culpability, Paul signals to his audience that Gentiles have been accepted as members of Ideal Israel.

Accordingly, in 3.21–26 Paul sketches a conception of redemption that includes the Gentiles. 'Redemption' (3.24) has a wide range of meanings (Jewett 2006: 282–3; Longenecker 2016: 422–3), but within 'the Law and Prophets' (3.21), it refers to the deliverance of the people of God from slavery (e.g. Exod. 6.6; Deut. 9.26; 13.5) or from exile (e.g. Isa. 41.14; 43.14;

---

[1] The question can also be translated as 'What then, do we have a disadvantage?' For a survey of issues, see Jewett (2006: 256–7); Longenecker (2016: 352–3).

44.22–24). Redemption in this connection therefore denotes the insoluble bond of God the redeemer with the elect as expressed in the covenant (Ps. 111.9; 130.7–8). The starting point for redemption is the 'justice of God' (Rom. 3.21). Paul described the revelation of God's justice as a present, ongoing reality in 1.17 and here he describes it as 'being made manifest through the faithfulness of Jesus Christ' (3.21) and intended 'for all who have faith, for there is no distinction' (3.22). The distinction being erased is that between Jews and Gentiles, but to his Gentile audience, 'all who have faith' describes them perfectly. Likewise the charge of universal fallenness – 'all have sinned and fallen short of the glory of God' (3.23) – ostensibly applies to all humanity but is levelled specifically against the Gentiles. By placing all on the same plane, Paul makes it possible for Gentiles 'to become right' with God alongside Jews through the same 'free offer of his grace through the redemption that is in Christ Jesus' (3.24).

Next Paul makes use of an early confession (Dunn 1988a: 1.163–64; Longenecker 2016: 394–7) to discuss his other major theme, faith, which is necessary for the reception of God's justice (3.25–26). The pre-Pauline confession probably reads: '[Christ] God put forth as an atonement (*hilastērion*) in his blood, for sake of the passing of sins previously committed by the forbearance of God'. Atonement as forgiveness of sin is at variance with Paul's usual conception of atonement as reconciliation (2 Cor. 5.19, 21; Jewett 2006: 286). It is closer to the martyrology of *4 Maccabees*, which presents victims as 'a ransom for the sin of *our nation:* through the blood of those pious ones and the *atonement* (*hilastērion*) of their death divine providence delivered *Israel* that had been mistreated' (*4 Macc.* 17.21–22; Jewett 2006: 286). Here 'our nation' and 'Israel' are objects of divine rescue. To this early confession, Paul inserts 'through faith' between 'atonement' and 'in his blood', making it a stand-alone comment on how Christ's atonement in his blood must be appropriated by Gentiles *through faith*.[2] That would provide support for his central idea that God's justice is disclosed 'through the faithfulness of Jesus Christ for all who have faith' (Rom. 3.22). This reference to both Christ's faithfulness and our faith is neatly summarized in the phrase 'one who issues from (literally, "one out of") the faithfulness of Jesus' (3.26). By zeroing in on the double reference of faith, Paul is able

---

[2] 'Faith in (*en*) his blood' has no parallel in Paul's letters and 'God put forth [Christ Jesus] as an atonement through faith' makes little coherent sense.

to expand the boundaries of 'our nation' and 'Israel' to include anyone who enters Ideal Israel through Christ's faithfulness. This universality is an invitation extended to Gentiles who can now accept it 'through faith' (3.25).

Faith, however, means obedience not work. It is not an action that merits reward but its opposite, an abandonment of self-prerogatives. That means Gentiles are accepted into God's covenant in the same way Jews are – by election. There is no room for boasting (3.27–31). Protestant interpreters often take the boasters (3.27) as Jews, but the profile here fits Gentile converts like a glove. They are identical to the hypercritics of 2.1–3.8 (Thorsteinsson 2003: 240) who suffer from two opposing complexes. On the one hand, they yearn to be considered Jewish and be included in the covenant because of their conversion. On the other hand, they overcompensate by stressing their accomplishments such as their circumcision, supercilious obedience to the law, and especially upholding the congregation in the absence of Jewish leaders.

To address these concerns, Paul states explicitly: 'Is God of the Jews only? No! Of the Gentiles also? Yes, also of the Gentiles, if indeed God is one' (3.29–30). The ground for including the Gentiles is the *shema*, the very foundation of Jewish monotheism (3.30). He then reminds the converts that faith means obedient acceptance of God's free offer of entrance into the covenant. Membership in Ideal Israel is not and cannot be secured by achievements but is only granted by divine election. Since the same offer is made to Jews as well, there is no distinction between Jews and Gentiles. Only in this context can we understand the enigmatic phrase 'law of faith' (3.27), an oxymoron for those who find law and faith incompatible. But his promotion of good work and his relatively positive evaluation of circumcision should convince us that Paul in no way rejects the law. At the conclusion of this section he states in no uncertain terms that faith does not invalidate the law; on the contrary, 'we uphold the law' (3.31). What he rejects is the notion that standing in the covenant could be earned when it is all the result of grace. Yes, Paul rejects legalism, but it is legalism practiced by Gentile converts who take pride in their accomplishments. The law is fulfilled not by stressing one's accomplishments ('law of works', 3.28) but by surrendering oneself to God's faithfulness ('law of faith', 3.27). Jews and Gentiles are placed on the same basis for accepting God's offer (3.29–30). There is no distinction; God shows no partiality and God has the absolute freedom to be God. These verses anticipate the full discussion of the same theme in chapters 9–11.

Abraham Father of All (4.1–25)

To cement his argument that Gentiles have a place in Ideal Israel, Paul provides an exegetical proof from Abraham. Whereas in Gal. 3.6–29 he was concerned with convincing Gentiles they were 'seed of Abraham', here he is persuading over-eager converts their achievements are no cause for pride. In calling Abraham '*our* forefather' (Rom. 4.1), Paul reminds his Gentile readers he is the superior rabbi instructing catechumens in his area of expertise. He speaks as the insider, a Jew by birth, natural heir of Abraham, mystagogue for the initiates.[3]

Paul returns to Physical Israel in order to draw out its implications for Ideal Israel. He begins by showing, because Abraham believed by surrendering himself in obedience, he was accepted into the covenant. The initiative lay with God's election alone (Gen. 15.6), not with Abraham's accomplishments (Rom. 4.2–5). In fact, God chose Abraham while he was 'impious' (4.5), before his conversion from polytheism to monotheism. At this point, Paul reaches his destination: Abraham the first convert was blessed while he was uncircumcised or, literally, while he was 'in foreskin' (4.10). It was only after the covenant had been established, according to Genesis 17, that Abraham 'received a sign of circumcision as a seal of the righteousness of his in-foreskin faith' (4.11). Circumcision is thereby reduced to an external seal of approval stamped on the covenant after the fact. More determinative is the substance of covenantal righteousness granted as a result of his self-surrendering faith while he was still uncircumcised.

Abraham's example thus embodies the common goal of the covenant, which Paul summarizes in two parallel statements. Abraham became 'the father of all who have faith through their uncircumcision', but he is also 'the father of circumcision' (4.11–12). This is the logical answer to the question raised earlier in diatribe form: 'Is this blessedness on the circumcision or also on the uncircumcision?' (4.9). The common approach is to take uncircumcision and circumcision as circumlocutions for Gentiles and Jews, but Paul the catechist might well use 'circumcision' to refer to the rite itself and 'uncircumcision' literally as 'foreskin': Abraham is the father of all *Gentiles* who have not circumcised but who 'have faith through their foreskin' (4.11) and all those who have circumcised. Abraham is 'the father of circumcision'

---

[3] See Hays (1985) for a detailed discussion of the difficult syntax of Rom. 4.1.

to those who have gone through the full conversion of circumcision, but he is also the father to those who follow his 'in-foreskin faith' (4.12).

Circumcision is therefore no longer the deciding question; trust in God is. The covenant has always been intended to benefit God's elect when received through obedience. From the start Physical Israel always implies Ideal Israel, and membership into Ideal Israel is determined not by physicality or ethnicity, not by distinguishing between Jews and Gentiles, but by surrendering to divine election that is independent of tribal distinctions, ethnic specificities, group prejudices. Far from an abstract doctrinal nicety, 'justification by faith' turns out to be a social principle of inclusion that cuts through all distinctions based on human artifice and prejudice (4.13–16). That principle applies 'not only to those who belong to the law but also to those who belong to the faith of Abraham who is the father of us all' (4.16).

Paul includes in the last third of the chapter (4.17–25) a topic that seems to have little to do with the foregoing, the trust of Abraham and Sarah in a God 'who makes the dead alive and calls non-beings into being' (4.17). But this passage allows Paul to segue to Christ, his resurrection, and eschatology, topics that will occupy Romans 5–8. The familiar story of an heir, Isaac, born to Abraham and Sarah at their old age is now given a new twist. Childlessness is compared to death, as signified by Abraham's advanced age and the 'deadness' of Sarah's womb (4.19), and birth is recast as resurrection (4.24–25). As Abraham was granted his promise through his steadfast faith, Gentiles are granted covenantal status by faith in a God 'who raised Jesus our Lord from the death'. But since Jesus is appointed cosmic Son of God through the resurrection, the covenantal people who are formed at that moment acquire a cosmic identity.

Paul naturally sees Abraham not in the abstract but only through the lens of Christ's resurrection. That is why he can claim the words 'it was reckoned to him [i.e., Abraham] unto righteousness' (4.22) are written not only for his sake but also for ours (4.23–24). 'Christ was delivered for sake of our transgressions and raised for sake of our justification' (4.25). But if fulfilment of the Abrahamic promise is framed exclusively in terms of Christ's resurrection, an intolerable problem immediately presents itself: What about the physical descendants of Abraham who came out of Isaac? Is Ideal Israel in danger of replacing Physical Israel? This question, to be answered in Romans 9–11, is what drives Paul to consider the deeper character of the covenant in the next four chapters.

The Peaceable Israel (Romans 5–8)

In these four chapters Paul builds a foundation for an Ideal Israel that incorporates their erstwhile enemies Gentiles. At the base of that foundation is Ideal Israel's claim to universality, a constant theme in the first four chapters of Romans. Paul presents his mission as winning the 'obedience of faith among *all* Gentiles' (1.5), which justifies his visit to the capital to bear some fruit among the Romans as 'among the rest of the Gentiles' (1.13). He revisits the promise given to Abraham that he will 'inherit the world' (4.13). Most prominent is his insistence that 'Jews and Gentiles' is a superior, more universal representation of humanity over against the Greco-Roman division of 'Greeks and barbarians' (1.14). But if that switch encodes a challenge to the Caesar-religion (see Chapter 1), the construction of Ideal Israel must embody an anti-imperial critique as well.

Upside-Down Peace (5.1–11)

These eleven verses form a bridge between the universal fatherhood of Abraham (4.1–25) and the unity of all humanity under New Adam (5.12–21), but they also introduce the larger section that reaches its climax in the new creation (chapter 8). The eschatological frame provided by these two bookends is visible in the transitional passage already: 'We will be saved… from the wrath' (5.9). It is in this eschatological context that we should understand boasting, which is otherwise rejected elsewhere in Romans (2.17, 23; 3.27; 4.2) but commended three times in this passage. Boasting 'in the hope of the glory of God' (5.2) looks forward to the future, as does boasting 'in our afflictions' (5.3), because it leads to hope (5.4). 'Boasting in God' (5.11) has an eschatological basis, because 'we received reconciliation' with God, the mark of the new creation (cf. 2 Cor. 5.17–21). Elsewhere Paul regards boasting as appropriate in the day of the Lord (2 Cor. 1.14; Phil. 2.16; 1 Thess. 2.19). Boasting in this regard is a natural result of confidence to stand before God in the end time (2 Cor. 3.12; Phil. 1.20). Shame (Rom. 5.5; 'disappoint' NRSV) is its opposite. It is what one must endure at the end when one falls short (Jewett 2006: 563). It has puzzled some Protestant interpreters why Paul would imply justification is inferior to future salvation: 'If we have been justified now by his blood, how much more will we be saved from the wrath! For if while we were enemies we were reconciled to God through the death of his son, how much more will we, being reconciled, be saved by his life!' (Rom. 5.9–10). From the perspective of the new creation and the salvation of 'all Israel', however, justification and reconciliation are but intermediate steps towards the eschatological goal of saving the reconstituted people of God.

Several major themes to be explored in the next four chapters are encapsulated in the opening statement: 'Having been justified out of faith, therefore, we have peace with God through our Lord Jesus Christ, through whom also we have come to gain access into this grace, in which we stand and boast in hope of the glory of God' (5.1–2). His audience knows by now 'justified out of faith' is a shorthand for inclusion in the covenant as a result of God's faithfulness. The opening verb 'having been justified' uses a divine passive to set the tone for the section: Inclusion depends exclusively on God's active agency.

Evidence points to Paul using Roman political-theological language to present God in this passage. *Prosagōgē* ('access', 5.2) appears only here among the genuine letters of Paul. It is both political and cultic. On the one hand, it refers to 'the unhindered access to the sanctuary as the place of God's presence' (Käsemann 1980: 133), and that is how the cognate verb *prosagein* ('to gain access') is used in the Septuagint (Lev. 4.14; Exod. 29.48, etc.) and in the Dead Sea Scrolls (1QS 11.13–15; 1QH 12.20–26). On the other hand, the word is also used to describe approach to a king (Xenophon, *Cyropaedia* 7.5.45; Longenecker 2016: 557–8). This separation between cult and court is a post-Enlightenment development, however, and does not reflect the political theology of Rome, where the two worked hand in glove (Dunn 1988a: 1.248). In fact, Caesar-religion was where this language was used (Jewett 2006: 350 citing Michael Wolter). Caesar-religion is also where we should look for the unPauline phrase '[standing] in this grace' (5.2). Grace as a space or realm to which one has access finds no parallel in Paul, who takes grace to be an extension of God's power to human beings. In an inscription dated to 68 CE, the expression 'the grace of god Claudius' (Dittenberger 1970: 669.28–29) was used in the imperial cult. 'Grace' was 'a fixed term for demonstrations of a ruler's favour' (Conzelmann 1974: 375) and refers to the 'beneficent dispensations of the emperor' (BDAG 2000: 1079). 'Having peace' (5.1) is likewise a common political slogan from early on (Xenophon, *Hellenica* 3.4.6.7; Demosthenes *Orationes* 12.22; Jewett 2006: 349), but it was the Romans who weaponized it to achieve military success. As expressed by Virgil, with heavy irony, it is the responsibility of Rome 'to pacify, to impose the rule of law, to spare the conquered, to battle down the proud' (*Aeneid* 6.852–53; see discussion in Chapter 1). Paul condemns *pax Romana* in 1 Thess. 5.3, where he consigns those who cry 'peace and security' (Latin *pax et securitas*) to destruction at the coming of the Son. The slogan was part of standard propaganda in early Imperial Rome (Koester 1997: 161–2).

Paul mimics imperial propaganda only to subvert it. The reason is that the means by which God's peace is achieved turns the imperial discourse on its head. Instead of 'pacifying' the world by means of violence and conquest, the Son of the God achieves peace and reconciliation by dying for his enemies: 'For while we were still weak, Christ died for the impious at the right time' (Rom. 5.6). The basis for Paul's language is a traditional creed: 'Christ died for us while we were still sinners' (5.8; Longenecker 2016: 563–4). But he immediately turns it into a political-theological statement: 'we were reconciled to God through the death of his son, *while we were enemies*' (Rom. 5.10). In the felicitous words of Dieter Georgi,

> Christ associates himself with a company of chaotic anarchists and rebels. He becomes a strange first among equals, a very singular sort of *princeps*. The ruler of the world joins company with those in rebellion against him… Romans 5:6-8 turns martyrdom into a death that establishes solidarity with the rebel and the enemy. This view of martyrdom protests the one-sided understanding of loyalty which prevailed in contemporary social and political life. There, loyalty means first and foremost the loyalty of subjects to their rulers. Paul declares an end to the deadly cycle of power, privilege, law, justice, and violence.
>
> (Georgi 1991: 97)

The peace through the death and resurrection of the cosmic Son of God makes nonsense of *Pax Romana*. Whoever heard of peace and reconciliation accomplished by the ruler joining company with his rebels! But that is exactly the upside-down peace brought about by Christ's death.

Christ the New Humanity (5.12–21)

Within this larger eschatological framework in which the future salvation of all Israel and the Roman imperium are all intertwined, Paul begins an extensive exploration of what that means for his Gentile converts. He does so by writing a history from the advent of New Adam to the completion of the new creation. There are two reasons why Adam is chosen. First, if Paul were to start a new Judaism, it would make better sense to present Christ as a new Moses, for Moses was known as the lawgiver *par excellence*. Instead, as New Adam, Christ becomes a healing agent to repair a broken world by engendering a new humanity (Rom. 5.12). If the object is all humanity, there is no reason to confine Christ to any one ethnic group, for inasmuch as sin and death have lorded over the world since Adam, New Adam's life-giving power will affect all humanity, both Jews and Gentiles. Second, New Adam is an eschatological figure. As Adam gave birth to all who are subject to death (5.12–14), Christ gives birth to all who will be raised in the same way that he was (cf. 1 Cor. 15.20–22).

The comparison between Adam's regime and New Adam's is inexact. Using an *a fortiori* argument, Paul concludes that the regime of grace is far superior to the regime of trespass: 'But the free gift is not like the trespass, for if all died because of the trespass of the one man, how much more did the grace of God and the gift in the grace of the one man Jesus Christ abound for all!' (5.15). The same idea is repeated using the same formula, 'if …, how much more … ', in 5.17. The verb 'to abound' (*perisseuein*) in Pauline usage carries the sense of overflowing to the point of removing 'boundaries or limitations' (Jewett 2006: 381). The regime of grace is different from the regime of trespass, therefore, not just because of its moral superiority but because old limitations can no longer hold the free gift of grace from breaking through its antiquated boundaries to inundate all. 'Many' (*polys*) is a Greek idiom for 'all'. The regime of grace is characterized by its surplus of generosity to all children of Adam and Eve.

That Paul compares the two regimes side by side shows that Christ's regime has not replaced Adam's but competes with it in real time. New Adam represents the beginning of the end, but the final chapter will not be written until creation is fully renewed. In the meantime, the two regimes exist side by side in an epic Manichean struggle while we are caught in between: 'Just as Sin exercises dominion through death, so Grace exercise dominion through righteousness for life eternal through Jesus Christ our Lord' (5.21). Under these conditions, this is our existential struggle: We must choose daily to whom we pledge our fealty – to Death (5.14, 17) or Sin (5.21; 6.12), which lords over (*basileuein*, literally 'to be king') Adam's regime; or to Grace (5.21), which lords over New Adam's regime. This mythic duel between Sin and Grace might strike one as an unsatisfactory conclusion to the Christ-Adam comparison, but because it was at the resurrection when Christ was installed as New Adam, the outcome is never in doubt. The new creation is in train and the final victory is assured by the very nature of that appointment.

In this cosmic drama, the law plays an ironic role. Sin gains power when it is named (5.13): 'The law came in, in order that the trespass might multiple' (5.20a). The use of the purpose clause is intentional. The law is introduced to limit Sin, but it also gives Sin a body and trespass goes viral. Still, 'where sin abounds, grace abounds all the more' (5.20b). Not only will New Adam be able to undo the damage inflicted on the world by Old Adam, he will surpass him in fulfilling the original promise of creation.

Mirroring the mythical battle between Old Adam and New Adam is a competition between Christ's realm and Caesar's. Augustus and his successors contend that Roman emperors embody a new humanity by inaugurating a new age (Latin *saeculum*). The Roman 'new age' is characterized by peace in the land and a golden age of prosperity and fertility. All this Paul consigns to Old Adam's regime of decay and death, while he names Christ as a superior benefactor: 'Jesus is what the *princeps* claimed to be: representative of humanity, reconciler and ruler of the world. Jesus is all this because he demonstrates the association and identification of God with those in rebellion against God' (Georgi 1991: 99–100).

Life between Emperors (6.1–23)

Caught between the regimes of Adam and Christ, we foot soldiers must decide under whose banner to enlist our service. This chapter is introduced with a typical diatribal question, 'What then shall we say? "Let us remain in sin in order that grace may abound"?' (Rom. 6.1). The question introduces a serious choice between Life and Death: 'How can those who have died to Sin still live in it?' (6.2). We have died to Sin, because at baptism 'we are baptized into his death' (6.3). Riffing on the double meaning of *baptizesthai*, literally 'to drown [as in a shipwreck]' (Liddell-Scott-Jones 1968: 305), Paul reinterprets baptism as identification with Christ's death and burial (Stendahl 1995: 27). Paul's thinking here is 'imperial' in that 'no one can serve two empires or masters simultaneously' (Jewett 2006: 396). If this binarism necessitates choosing one regime over another, dying with Christ means disavowing the regime of Sin and 'a change of lordship' (Tannehill 1967: 18). Baptism means declaring the lordship of Christ and renouncing all other forms of lordship.

If, however, Christ is presented as a superior alternative to the idyllic *saeculum* of Augustus and Nero, then choosing Christ over Sin or anyone that challenges Christ's lordship is surely no mere religious devotion but requires that one forsake the lordship of Caesar. Whether one could remain in Sin then is no longer a hypothetical question but is raised to challenge those wishing to maintain their standing in the Caesar-religion while pledging their allegiance to Christ. Paul's answer is a resounding 'By no means!' (6.2). Paul does not equate the regime of Sin to Caesar's rule explicitly; eyes of the imperial censors are sharp. But insofar as Paul sets them both in opposition to Christ's regime in a binary construction, dying with Christ must mean forsaking Caesar or any government that demands our commitment to the lordship of Christ be replaced and displaced by absolute obedience to an earthly ruler. In his apocalyptic mindset which rejects all earthly authorities and powers (Elliott 1997a: 176–81), Paul feels no compulsion to keep Sin and the Caesar-religion distinct. Now it becomes clear why Paul stresses on identifying with Christ's death and makes no mention of identifying with his resurrection (Rom. 6.3). Dying with Christ requires a renunciation of regimes consigned to this decaying order.

While Paul is definitive on the sacramental power of baptism tying us to Christ's death, he does not take the final step in claiming we have been raised. That will happen only in the future. Whenever both death and resurrection are mentioned, the comparison follows a consistent pattern:

Table 1 Dying and Rising in Romans 6.

	Dying	Rising
6.4	We have been buried	We walk in newness of life
6.5	We identify in likeness of his death	We will identify with his resurrection
6.8	If we have died with Christ	We believe we will live with him
6.11	Consider yourselves dead	[Consider yourselves] living for God

Death and burial are presented as past events, while rising with Christ is described either as a future occurrence or as a commitment for action. The Paul of Romans 6 displays none of the certitude of his disciple who proclaims, 'we have been raised with Christ!' (Col. 3.1). One reason for Paul's reservation is his experience with the Corinthian enthusiasts, but the immediate reason is the constant pressure the Caesar-religion exerts on the congregation. He is only too aware of the impact the expulsion of leaders has had on this community. The defeat of the present regime, while assured, has yet to be realized in history. In the meantime, Paul is confident that death no longer rules over Christ (6.9), even though that condition does not yet obtain for those torn between two emperors. Christ's death and resurrection therefore presents a simple directive: 'Consider yourselves dead to Sin but living for God in Christ Jesus' (6.11).

Paul formulates this personal choice in cultic terms, thus making ethical responsibility into a constitutive element of worship (6.12–23). Life between emperors is a matter of religious devotion: 'Do not present your members as weapons of wickedness for Sin but present yourselves to God as if you were alive from the dead, and [present] your members as weapons of righteousness for God' (6.13). Identical language is used to speak of presenting one's body as a living sacrifice to God (12.1–2). The similarity is deliberate. Sin and Grace are presented as lords to whom we devote ourselves as slaves (6.16). Worship of God demands an ethical choice, and personal commitment to the absolute good stands at the heart of religious devotion. Worship and ethics are inextricably bound together. Left unsaid but understood by the audience is what that means to them in real time. If a regime with no legitimate claim to the absolute good nevertheless demands from us religious devotion, such a regime is a perversion of true worship. It is a regime of Sin that enslaves us with its law (6.14–15; cf. 5.20) – not the Mosaic law, as Paul's audience would know, but the promise of rewards in artifices and empty works. The regime of Sin installs itself as a false god and demands absolute loyalty from its subjects. It goes without saying that here Paul has in mind the regime that prides itself for its law.

The Law Is Law, and Sin Is Sin (7.1–25)

By railing against the 'law' in the last two chapters, Paul has painted himself into a corner. The Law of Moses is an irreducible part of Judaism, and if the Torah were sinful, what of the people of God and 'all Israel'? Paul's answer is that the Jewish law must be dissociated from Sin. The Torah is a written code incapable of generating life by itself, and Sin is a cosmic power capable of turning even the holy and good into deadly weapons. How does it achieve that? By mobilizing fleshly frailty.

Chapter 7 begins with an analogy from ancient marriage that capitalizes on the just-concluded theme of dying with Christ (7.1–6). Just as dying with Christ means a change of loyalty from one regime to another, a woman in the first century must subject herself to her husband, but his death would release her from the marriage contract. The analogy is inexact and creates more problems than it solves (Stendahl 1995: 27): it should have been *her* dying rather than her husband's that dissolves her legal obligations.

Discussion of the Jewish law begins in 7.7. Interpretation of 7.7–25 has been unduly dominated by the attempt to identify 'I', but the opening diatribe questions – 'What then shall we say? That the law is sin?' – supply a telling clue: Paul is primarily concerned with dissociating the Torah from Sin. Paul categorically denies the connection, but it is undeniable that the Torah furthers Sin's cause, unwittingly, by naming it: 'I did not know Sin except through the law, for I would not have known covetousness if the law had not said "Do not covet"' (7.7). By giving substance to fleshly impulses, the Torah is co-opted by Sin to devastating effects, in spite of its impeccable pedigree. Thus Paul laments, 'the commandment which [was given] for life, this is death to me. So I died' (7.10). But Paul insists that 'the law is holy, and the commandments are holy, just, and good' (7.12). It is Sin, seizing the peculiar nature of the law, that deceives and kills (7.11, 13).

To illustrate Sin's ability to insinuate itself into our lives and our struggle with it, Paul constructs a soliloquy or what first-century rhetoricians called a 'speech-in-character' (*prosopopoeia*; 7.14–25; see Stowers 1994: 264–9 for discussion). In spite of the use of 'I', the speech is intended not as an autobiography but as an exposition on the existential struggle we face torn between two empires. We yearn to follow the holy and spiritual law of God, but the law of Sin enslaves us and pulls us in the opposite direction (7.22–23). The result is a classic statement on our human inability to do what we desire: 'So then, I myself am a slave in my mind to the law of God, but in my flesh [a slave] to the law of sin!' (7.25).

The New Creation (8.1–39)

The pessimistic note that ends chapter 7 paves the way for a triumphant acclamation: 'There is now no condemnation for those who are in Christ!'

(8.1). Thus begins the new creation, the climax towards which the struggle between Adam and Christ builds. The struggle sweeps up everyone in its wakes and insinuates itself into our daily life, but its ultimate resolution will bring Paul's anti-imperial critique to new heights by rejecting the foundation of Roman political theology, the supposed unity between Caesar and nature.

The first topic, flesh *versus* spirit (8.1–17), is a continuation of the last chapter, except the terminology is now changed to 'the law of the spirit of life in Christ Jesus' *versus* 'the law of sin and death' (8.2). This harks back to the earlier contrast between the law of works that fails and the law of faith that succeeds (3.27). Here Christ's incarnation and death are taken to be the means by which 'God judged Sin in the flesh, in order that the righteous deed of the law might be fulfilled in those of us who walk not in the flesh but in the spirit' (8.3–4). In setting the opposition as Christ *versus* Sin, the law is left off from the debate. The law is hopelessly 'weakened through the flesh'; it can offer no help of its own. The just requirements can be fulfilled only by those who follow the life of the spirit (8.4). The reason for bringing the incarnation into this discussion is left unspoken, but the context makes it clear that it is because Christ was born 'in the likeness of the flesh of sin', his death can be construed as a defeat of Sin and Flesh. Correspondingly, Christ's resurrection inaugurates a life in the spirit (8.5–8) and creates an escape from the existential despair of chapter 7: namely, to conduct oneself in accordance with the Spirit of God, who dwells within (8.9).

In midst of a discussion on life in the spirit, Paul takes an unexpected turn to the body: 'If Christ is in you, then the body is dead on account of sin, but the *Spirit* is life on account of righteousness' (8.10). 'Spirit' refers to the eschatological 'Spirit that raised Jesus from the dead' (8.11). If that Spirit dwells within, it can revive the mortal body (8.11). Paul makes use of dualistic language of flesh and spirit but honours the body. We are, therefore, faced with a choice: either to live by the flesh and die (8.12–13a) or to live by the Spirit and be granted adoption as children of God (8.13b–17).

The struggle between flesh and spirit comes to a denouement in the eschaton. The end is just like the beginning, except better. The present sufferings cannot be compared to 'the glory about to be revealed *into us*' (8.18). The odd prepositional phrase indicates a 'marker of goal' (BDAG 2000: 290): the future glory is revealed to as far as us as its aim, 'so that we become the actual partakers' (Jewett 2006: 510). Creation is personified to such a degree that it can be described as anticipating in 'eagerly expectation' the disclosure of the sons of God (Jewett 2006: 511), with the implication that the saints will help creation reach its goals (8.19). The creation depicted here includes human beings but also all sentient beings and inanimate objects; it is a living organism marked by agency and purpose. Like children of First Adam, it is subject to decay and death, but unlike them, it is subjected involuntarily 'by the one who subjected it' (8.20). Creation itself looks forward to its own liberation from the 'slavery of decay' (8.21a) but with a purpose (the preposition 'into' again): namely, 'the liberation of the glory of the children of God' (8.21b). Both creation and all sentient beings join together for mutual assistance and for liberation as the glory of God is revealed. Even though the new creation is realized through divine initiative, neither creation nor human beings are depicted as passive bystanders. They are active participants and eager partakers, making them primary stakeholders in creation. They stand to gain in arresting the corruption that subjects the world to decay: 'For we know that the whole creation is groaning [with us] in labor pains until now; not only that but we ourselves, with the spirit as the first fruits, also groan among ourselves while we wait for adoption, the redemption of our body' (8.22–23).

This picture of the world groaning for liberation from decay is a far cry from the Roman portrait of nature as an idyllic reflection of *pax Romana* (Georgi 1991: 100–1). Virgil proclaims Augustus to be the son of god who will inaugurate a new age, the 'Age of Saturn', a return to the lost golden age (*Aeneid* 6.789–94; Jewett 2004: 27). In his *Carmen saeculare* composed for the secular games of 17 BCE, Horace celebrates Augustus's victory as the salvation of the republic by 'a return of the golden age and paradise' (Georgi 1997: 41; Jewett 2004: 28). Nero is also said to have ushered in a 'golden age of untroubled peace' (Jewett 2006: 517). Most iconic is the fulsome image of Mother Earth on Augustus's Peace Altar allegorizing fertility, fecundity, and peace. These accounts portray the emperor as the long-awaited saviour responsible for the restoration of nature to its pristine Hesiodic golden age. Even 'the age-old virtues of *pietas, pax, honor,* and *virtus* have returned' (Georgi 1997: 42; Elliott 2008: 121–61).

By contrast, Paul depicts nature as chaotic and subjected to death and corruption, itself yearning to collaborate with the children of God for redemption. Against Roman propaganda, he rejects the notion that creation could determine the success of the imperial order or that powerful emperors could redeem it. Paul does indeed look forward to renewal, but that remains a future event to be fulfilled only through the extraordinary sacrifice of the Son of God taking on sinful flesh (Rom. 8.3–4). The emperors bring about their empty *pax* by laying waste of enemies and nature in pursuit of military victories. Paul's new creation relies on mutual cooperation between creation and humanity when both are subjected to atrophy, decay, and death. Robert Jewett's summary of the differences between the Genesis story of creation and Roman mythology is apt: 'In this powerful symbolization [in Genesis], humans trying to play God ended up ruining not only their relations with each other but also their relation to the natural world. The Roman myth system claimed the exact opposite: that a ruler who plays god can restore the world to a paradisiacal condition by his piety and military dominance' (Jewett 2006: 513).

The new creation is, therefore, an unfinished product, even as we are torn between regimes. What gives hope is that the eschatological Spirit, which we have as 'first-fruits' (Rom. 8.23), provides verification that the new creation has been inaugurated and daily reminder that it will come to full fruition. The Spirit accomplishes this by accompanying those of us who 'sigh deeply to ourselves while we eagerly wait for adoption, the redemption of our body' (8.23) and by interceding for us with 'wordless sighs' (8.26–27). But unlike the imperial promise, those whom God called (8.29–30) have a personal stake in the new creation and must actively participate in its realization, because 'in all things [the Spirit] works *together* with those who love God' (8.28). Allegiance to the New Adam entails a privilege as children and an obligation as stakeholders to fulfil the promises of the new creation.

Paul ends the section in a triumphant yet defiant note (8.31–39). He begins in typical diatribe fashion: 'What then shall we say? If God is for us, who is against us?' (8.31), but his follow-up discussion two verses down makes it clear that Paul has in mind specific cases. The questions, 'Who will bring any charge against God's elect?… Who is the condemner?' (8.33, 34), have their natural home in a court of law. They are posed here to assure his audience that they will not be abandoned to the vagaries of imperial censors. Paul's answers must therefore be understood against that context. Who will bring charges against the elect? If it is 'God who justifies' the accused (8.33), then the imperial authorities do not. Who will condemn God's people? If it is 'Christ who died and, indeed, raised, who is at the right hand of God, who intercedes for us' (8.34), the selfsame Christ whose resurrection defeated the death sentence imposed upon him by the Empire, then surely the same imperial authorities are powerless to condemn God's elect. Nothing can separate us from the love of Christ, not 'affliction, distress, persecution, hunger, nakedness, danger, or sword' (8.35).

Has God Rejected Israel?
(Romans 9–11)

The focus on Ideal Israel and the place of Gentiles in it creates a problem for Paul: What of Physical Israel? The covenant was established with historic Israel, out of which the Messiah came, yet the Jesus-movement has failed to attract Jewish followers. If the original people of the covenant are abandoned and replaced, what guarantees that the new people will not one day be abandoned as well? God is free to elect whomever to the covenant; no human achievement merits election. What at first appears to be a demographic problem quickly becomes a theological crisis centring on God's faithfulness. The lack of precision in Paul's language also contributes to the problem. He regards Gentile converts as full members of the covenant with its rights and privileges. Throughout chapters 5–8, for example, Paul refrains from treating them as Gentiles outside the covenant. In dealing with Physical Israel in chapters 9–11, however, Paul reverts to the old distinction between Jews and Gentiles established in chapters 1–4.

Paul begins by professing his love for his own people, members of Physical Israel, and the pride for the privilege they enjoy:

> There is great pain and unceasing sorrow in my heart. For I pray that I myself be damned from Christ on behalf of my brothers and sisters, my kinsfolk according to the flesh, who are Israelites, to whom belong the adoption, the service, and the promises; to whom belong the patriarchs and from whom came the Christ according to the flesh. May the God of all be blessed forever, Amen.
>
> (9.2–5)

In so doing he reminds his audience the vantage point he assumes throughout Romans, that of a pedagogue guiding novices through the subtleties of the Jesus-movement. Here he signals that he will speak on behalf of his own kinsfolk and, if need be, assume an adversarial position towards the Gentiles. The question implicit in this autobiographical statement is explicitly raised in 11.1: Has God forsaken the original people of the covenant?

The Absolute Freedom of God (9.6–10.21)

The first part of Paul's answer (9.6–29) proves from Scripture God's absolute freedom to choose whomever to fulfil divine objectives. Citing Hosea, 'Jacob

I loved, but Esau I hated' (9.13), Paul suggests that God made the selection 'before they were born or did anything good or bad' (9.11). The upshot is that it is within God's prerogatives to include Gentiles as much as Jews. In fact, Paul envisions only a 'remnant chosen by grace' (11.5) is in a position to seed Ideal Israel, because 'not all who issue from [Physical] Israel are [Ideal] Israel, nor are all children the seed of Abraham' (9.6–7).

Election creates inequity, however, at least from the human standpoint, but Paul resorts to a restatement of faith *versus* works for solution:

> What then shall we say, that Gentiles who did not pursue righteousness received righteousness, the righteousness of faith, while Israel, in pursuing a law of righteousness did not attain it. Why? Because [they pursue it] not out of faith but as through works.
>
> (9.30–32)

Here faith and works refer not to personal salvation but, as before, represent two contrasting approaches to reconstituting God's people. Works represent a reliance on human distinctions and achievements to forge group identity, while faith represents a trust in God's election, which could entail the movement, redefinition, even erasure of boundaries to include the formerly excluded. That is the context in which to understand Paul's critique of his own kinsfolk: 'For I testify on their behalf that they have a zeal for God but without any genuine knowledge; being ignorant of God's justice and seeking to establish their own, they did not submit to God's justice' (10.2–3). God's justice means opening the covenant to include born Gentiles, and resistance to that idea is what constitutes ignorance.

Paul does not reject Physical Israel; his autobiographical preface in 9.2–5 makes that abundantly clear. Instead, he is responding to the charge that the Jesus-movement, in receiving Gentiles in record number, represents inequity to Israel when the constitution of Israel herself was due to God's election. In resisting the inclusion of Gentiles, intransigent Israel is violating the founding spirit of the covenant, God's freedom. Accordingly we are in a better position to understand the long-debated line: 'For the end (*telos*) of the law is Christ for justice to everyone who has faith' (10.4). Like 'end', *telos* could mean either 'cessation or termination' or 'goal'. It is unlikely Paul means Christ replaces the Torah, for nowhere does he advocate that the law be abandoned, whereas throughout Romans, Paul consistently stresses the oracular nature of the Torah and its holiness. It seems more accurate to take Christ to be the 'conclusion or climax' of the Torah given the ethnic context on Jews and Gentiles. Just as Ideal Israel is embodied in Physical Israel when Abraham was selected patriarch, Christ is also embodied in the Torah. In support of this view, Paul cites from Scripture to demonstrate how the Torah points to Christ (10.5–21). Regarding righteousness that comes from the law, 'the person who does [the commandments] will live by them' (10.5), citing Lev. 18.5. The verse is often taken as criticism against Israel's supposed inability to fulfil the law, but Paul's language is in fact different. Instead of contrasting works to faith, he is concerned more with demonstrating how righteousness that comes from faith points to Christ (Rom. 10.6–8). Properly executed, the Torah leads to Christ.

After another string of citations from Scripture to demonstrate the necessity of faith for all (10.9–18), Paul returns to the present and future status of Physical Israel. Three biblical texts serve as basis. From Deut. 30.21 Paul finds proof that the current waywardness of Israel must be seen in light of Gentile acceptance: 'I will make you jealous of a non-people, with a foolish people I will anger you' (10.19). A second text, Isa. 65.1, is identical in affirmation: 'I have been found by those who did not seek me, and I became known to those who did not ask for me' (10.20). Paul cites these two passages not to show God has forsaken Israel but to demonstrate that God is in charge and has only Israel's welfare in mind. Even though Israel has shown itself to be 'a people disobedient and contrary', it has always been and will continue to be the centre of God's attention. This the third text, Isa. 65.2, makes clear: 'All day long I extended my hand' to them (Rom. 10.21). In sum, it is all about Israel even when it appears to have wandered away from the straight and narrow.

Jews and Gentiles in Ideal Israel (11.1–24)

Now that the context is set, Paul raises his question explicitly: 'Has God rejected his people?' (11.1). As before (9.1–5), he recites his own credentials in Physical Israel, 'I am an Israelite, from the seed of Abraham and tribe of Benjamin' (11.1), to restate his position as the superior rabbi before introducing his notion of 'remnant', which will seed a reform of Physical Israel (11.5) despite its momentary failure to attain what it seeks (11.7–10).

The concept of the remnant is well known in biblical literature and in Qumran (Jewett 2006: 659). Its basic idea is that a small group representing the true interests of Israel will be saved, as shown by Isa. 10.22: 'Even though the number of the children of Israel are like sand of the sea, [only] the *remnant* will be saved' (Rom. 9.27). That idea is also found in the *Damascus Document* 1.3–13: the Babylonian conquest destroyed only the wicked but spared a 'remnant' who repented of their sins (cited in Jewett 2006: 659). But the remnant could also act as agents of reform, sowing seeds that will result in the restoration of all Israel. So the remnant will be restored to their own land to populate it according to Jer. 23.3: 'Then I myself will gather the remnant of my flock out of all the lands where I have driven them, and I will bring them back to their fold, and they shall be fruitful and multiply' (NRSV). That appears to be the meaning Paul attaches to the oracular answer to Elijah: 'I have left for myself seven thousand men who have not bent their knees to Baal' (Rom. 11.4 citing 1 Kings 19.18). For while the Scriptural citations in 11.7–10 seem to support that the majority of Israel has resisted in their obstinacy, its stumbling is temporary by design. It is because of their trespasses that 'salvation [came] to the Gentiles – in order to provoke them to jealousy' (11.11). Inasmuch as their stumbling has contributed to riches to the world and to the Gentiles, 'how much more will their fulfilment (*plērōma*) be!' (11.12). *Plērōma* is misleadingly translated as 'full inclusion' in the NRSV, as if Israel had been excluded from the covenant but would be re-admitted in some future date. A better translation is to take it either literally as 'fullness' or as 'fulfilment' (BDAG 2000: 829–30), a condition contrasted to its current condition as 'loss' (*hēttēma*, NRSV 'defeat'). The return of Israel will be the completion of a predestined plan intended from the start of the covenant.

But whom does Paul call the 'remnant'? He includes himself, no doubt, and Jews like him committed to the Jesus-movement. If biblical tradition holds, he likely includes also unforeseen members of Israel who will play some part in the reconstitution of Israel. Beyond that, who else? The way Paul ties it to 'the election of grace' (11.5) provides a clue. 'Election' is used only four times in Romans, five in all of Paul's letters. It is twice applied to the election of Israel (9.11; 11.28) and twice to Gentiles. In 11.7, the 'elected' is contrasted to Israel; in Paul's earliest extant letter, it is used to refer to Gentile converts (1 Thess. 1.4). The only constant is that he firmly believes agency lies exclusively with God, in whose mysterious depths is the remnant formed (Longenecker 2016: 880–1). It is, therefore, futile to identify the remnant with any institution or group, not even the congregation to whom Paul is addressing. The combination of election and grace takes the identity of the remnant out of all human considerations and places it squarely in the realm of divine providence.

Once Paul reveals the future fate of Israel, he addresses his audience directly starting with Rom. 11.13. Up till now since the start of chapter 9, the Gentiles have been listening in, detached and uninvolved. To them, the fate of Physical Israel might seem abstract and distant, but in fact the discussion was constructed for their benefit. The payoff is when Paul forces his Gentile audience to contemplate their own place in the covenant. He addresses them, bluntly: 'To you I speak as Gentiles. Inasmuch as I myself am an apostle to the Gentiles, I glorify my service if somehow I provoke my own flesh to jealousy and save some of them' (11.13–14). If it has not become clear from his recounting of the Jewish prerogatives (9.2–5), he now makes it explicit that he sides with his kinsfolk ('flesh'). To put the Gentiles in their place, Paul allegorizes Ideal Israel as a cultivated olive tree in 11.17–24. The tree represents God's covenant with Israel, the domesticated branches, while Gentiles are nothing but 'wild olive branches', belatedly grafted onto the tree because some branches had been lopped off from the original. Paul then warns: 'It is not you who support the root but the root you' (11.18). Gentiles are 'by nature a wild olive branch [that has been], contrary to nature, grafted into a cultivated olive tree' (11.24). The same God who accepts the Gentiles into the covenant out of an extraordinary show of grace can likewise cut them off. There is therefore no basis for boasting, for one's place in Ideal Israel depends entirely on God's election. Gentiles are now members of a covenant they have no right to be a part of; their inclusion is a gift, not works or achievement.

Paul also reminds his Gentile audience that their inclusion is made possible by Physical Israel's momentary lapse; they have not displaced or replaced them and never will. God is not creating a new people *ex nihilo* to replace Physical Israel; Paul is not envisioning a 'third race' beyond Jews and Gentiles. Physical Israel in fact embodies Ideal Israel. Once the original occupants return, a prospect Paul not only allows for but in fact eagerly expects, they will resume mastery of the house. So what is the purpose of letting interlopers into Israel in the meantime? To provoke Physical Israel into jealousy so they may be saved. If their 'disobedience' has already meant blessings to the world, imagine how glorious it would be when they return to the fold.

'And so all Israel will be saved' (11.25–36)

And Israel will return, Paul assures his Gentile readers, and that is a mystery to be disclosed in the end time: 'For I do not want you to be ignorant, brothers and sisters, of this mystery, lest you [appear to be] wiser than you are: A hardening has come upon parts of Israel – until the fullness of Gentiles has come in. And so all Israel will be saved... ' (11.25–26). This is an extraordinary statement on the relation between Gentiles and Israel.

First, Paul affirms the irrevocability of God's promises to Israel, so the future redemption of Israel ('will be saved' refers to the end time) is not in doubt (11.26). Since through election God has established an eternal covenant with Israel, God will remain faithful and honour it to the end. Even when Israel might appear to be 'enemies of God', they are beloved because of the eternal promises made to the patriarchs (11.28).

Second, there are reasons for Jews and Gentiles to depend on each other. 'You yourselves (i.e., Gentiles) once disobeyed God but have now been given mercy because of their (i.e., the Jews') disobedience' (11.30). This sentiment is already expressed earlier in the olive tree allegory: Gentiles have been grafted onto the olive tree because some domestic branches had been broken off. But Israel's 'disobedience' is only temporary; it creates an opening for Gentiles. Physical Israel disobeyed not because of constitutional intransigency but as the result of a divine plan. Their momentary waywardness paves the way for a 'non-people' to become God's people. Gentile converts, therefore, have no grounds for boasting.

Third, who is the 'redeemer' in Paul's citation of Isa. 59.20–21?

Out of Zion will come the redeemer;
he will turn away impiety from Jacob.
And this is my covenant with them,
when I take away their sins.

(11.26–27)

It would dovetail with Paul's mission if the answer were Christ. But Paul's main concern at this stage of his argument is not how Gentiles have been granted entrance into the covenant but why *Jews* have been temporarily shut out of the Jesus-movement and how the people of the original covenant would find their way back. If so, 'my covenant' with Jacob can only refer to God's covenant with Israel, and 'redeemer' must retain its original reference to God. If God has temporarily excluded Israel through their 'disbelief', only God can reinstate them through divine election. Paul is envisioning salvation of Israel without the benefit of Christ! Paul covers himself by calling this a 'mystery', a secret to be uncovered in the end time (11.25).

Paul's citation of Isa. 59.20 in 11.26 includes several modifications. The most major is the change from the Hebrew 'To or for (*le*) Zion' or the Septuagint 'for sake of (*heneken*) Zion' to 'out of (*ek*) Zion'. Why does Paul feel obligated to reverse the direction of the redeemer's movement, describing him as coming out of Zion instead of going to it? It would appear that for Paul, Zion is not the object of deliverance but its starting point. It is the capital of Ideal Israel where the redeemer will launch his rescue operation. Here the new ethnic paradigm directly challenges political reality; for in the formation of Ideal Israel, its boundaries are now thrown wide open to include all Gentiles, thereby threatening to swallow up all earthly empires.

Character of the New Community (Romans 12–15)

In this last major section (12.1–15.13), Paul turns to the character of the New Community. The community is new in the eschatological sense: Paul and his audience were keenly aware the death and resurrection of Christ marked a turning point in God's dealing with humanity. Neither Paul nor his contemporaries understood fully the character of the New Community, how it was related to Ideal Israel, or what role it might play in God's covenant with Israel, but no one denied the relationship. Answers by students of a particular persuasion are found in the later epistles Colossians and Ephesians, but they should not be attributed to Paul. In the final analysis, it seems prudent to leave the indeterminate relationship between the New Community and Ideal Israel the way we find it in Romans.

Since Paul knew the Roman congregation only in general terms, he might have intended his responses to be relevant to other assemblies as well. Perhaps that is why, despite new topics (such as governing authorities in 13.1–7), he recycles materials from his other letters. The topic of spiritual gifts in the body of Christ, first introduced in 1 Corinthians 12–14, is developed further in Rom. 12.3–8. Eating meat as opposed to vegetable, first found in 1 Corinthians 10, is framed in more specific terms in Rom. 14.1–23. His apocalypticism was part of his proclamation to Gentiles from the earliest days (1 Thess. 4–5; 1 Cor. 15); it reappears here albeit with less vividness (Rom. 13.11–14).

Renewing the Collective Mind (12.1–2)

As anticipated in chapter 6, ethical life follows from religious devotion. Worship gives the New Community its identity and forms the basis for praxis:

I urge you, therefore, sisters and brothers, through the mercies of God to present your bodies as a sacrifice, living, holy, and pleasing to God – your rational worship. And do not be conformed to this age but be transformed by renewal of your mind, that you may ascertain what is the will of God – the good, pleasing, and perfect.

(12.1–2)

'I urge' (NRSV 'I appeal') translates more accurately the strong Greek verb *parakalō* and better reflects Paul's self-ascribed status as a superior rabbi to his Gentile audience. He does the same two verses later, where he underscores his teaching by referring to 'the grace that was given to me' (12.3). Presenting oneself as a sacrifice recalls the same language in 6.12–23 used in the pledging of allegiance to a sovereign. 'Rational worship' ('*spiritual* worship' in most modern translations) is closer to the Greek and more accurately reflects the common philosophical understanding that proper worship involves our rational faculty to the fullest (Dunn 1988b: 2.711; Jewett 2006: 729–30). It also goes better with the emphasis on the mind, which when renewed could help 'ascertain' the will of God on basis of reasoning (12.2).

Paul's audience would readily recognize sacrifice as a metaphor for personal devotion (Jewett 2006: 727). What is unique is Paul's appeal to communal mysticism when he says, 'to present your *bodies* as a sacrifice'. According to Jewett, 'in contrast to the "individualized mysticism of late antiquity" that spoke of replacing blood sacrifices with divine knowledge, virtue, and prayer, Paul refers here to the *collective* devotion of the Roman believers as a group' (Jewett 2006: 728; emphasis added). He does the same when he calls for a transformation based on reason. In this connection, the caution not to be 'conformed to this age' is most ominous, since this age, under Old Adam's reign, is occupied most prominently by the Roman Empire.

Inside-Out Love (12.3–13.14)

This communal mysticism takes shape in a 'body of Christ' (12.3–8). The topic enters into Pauline vocabulary first in 1 Corinthians: 'For just as the body is one and has many members and all the members of the body, though many, are one, so also Christ' (1 Cor. 12.12). With 'Christ' equated to 'body', Christ is the mystical body encompassing diverse members. Against dissension, Paul prescribes unity in the same spirit, the same Lord, the same

God (1 Cor. 12.4–6). In Romans, however, Paul singles out the individuals and stresses the diversity in the same body. Paul calls attention to the audience's individuality with a clumsy but effective phrase, 'to everyone who is among you', and places 'each' in an emphatic position (Rom. 12.3). The same body encompasses a diversity of practices: 'For just in one body we have many members, all the members do not have the same practice, so the many of us are one body in Christ and each one of us are members of one another' (12.4–5). Different members should be allowed to practice freely whatever gifts (*charismata*) they are given (12.6–8), for God has given each 'a measure (*metron*) of faith' (12.3). Since Paul never sees faith as something quantifiable, it is probably better to take the expression as meaning our measuring rod that takes as its starting point in our obedient relation to God.

'Genuine love' (12.9a) announces the main theme of this subsection (12.9–21). The phrase has no verb and can be translated with an imperatival force, 'Let love be genuine' (NRSV), or as a statement, 'love is without pretence' (Jewett 2006: 754). To honour its simple structure, I take it as a declarative label on which the whole sentence of 12.9b–13 hangs syntactically. In the same way the body of Christ in 1 Corinthians 12 segues to a statement on love as the most excellent gift (1 Cor. 12.31), Paul here follows the same pattern. But instead of relying on an ode to love (1 Cor. 13) to make his point, he develops a detailed theory of love that redefines the shape, character, even the boundaries of the New Community.

The love declaration is expanded into a two-way theology: 'abhorring the evil, embracing the good' (12.9b–c). The implication is that 'distinguishing between the "evil" and the "good" is the means by which love is kept "genuine"' (Jewett 2006: 760), but Paul makes the distinction in order to weaken it and eventually to erase it. That is because in the ensuing discussion, Paul uses 'good' and 'evil' not as moral terms but primarily as sociological categories demarcating insiders from outsider. What 'embracing good' means is immediately expanded in the following verse: 'devoting to one another in brotherly and sisterly love, holding each other in high esteem' (12.10). With the repetition of 'each other', Paul points to the ethos and ethics of the New Community, which are determined by genuine love. Accordingly, Paul lifts up zeal, fervency, hope, affliction, and prayer (12.11–12) not as personal virtues but as communal functions, as epitomized in the community concern of 'sharing the needs of the saints, pursue hospitality' (12.13). Paul consistently uses the verb *koinōnein* ('to share') to mean sharing of monetary resources (Rom. 15.27; Gal. 6.6; Phil. 4.15) and it is no different here. The

New Community is made up of resident aliens with a heavy tax burden in a network of squalid tenements (see Chapter 1). Members are now exhorted to share their resources with other members as they have needs.

With 'pursue hospitality' in the second half of 12.13b, Paul transitions to his explication of 'abhorring the evil'. *Philoxenia* ('hospitality', literally 'love of strangers') is a well-known virtue in Greek, Roman, and Jewish cultures, but what makes it unique here is its unqualified, absolute usage, with no restriction to ethnicity or association and no reference to reward. The paradigm of hospitality is Abraham's reception of the three angels (Gen. 18), but in contrast to Heb. 13.2, which mentions the episode, Paul makes no use of 'entertaining angels' as enticement. Instead, he chooses an aggressive verb, *diōkein* ('to pursue, to persecute'), to make hospitality an active goal. The New Community must pursue hospitality with 'vigorous intentionality' (Jewett 2006: 765), taking care to receive strangers and outsiders with no distinction and with no calculus of reward to motivate them. They do it because of the inherent goodness of hospitality. They do it because hospitality is the outflow of an authentic love.

Once we practice unconditional love towards strangers, however, the wall separating insiders from outsiders crumbles, differences between them is erased, enemies become indistinguishable from friends, and the rationale for enmity is called into question. Outside hostility against the New Community forms the main theme of the rest of chapter. Paul exhorts, 'Bless the persecutors, bless and not curse' (12.14). Paul uses the same verb *diōkein* here as he does in the last verse, thus consciously linking loving those who threaten us with hostility to the pursuit of hospitality towards strangers. Some manuscripts read 'Bless those who persecute *you*', making it a situational response in case of persecution, but Paul's injunction is broader and more absolute: Bless *any* persecutor and do not curse. At stake is not just knowing how to behave in the event of unjust aggression; at stake is the character of a New Community that is forged by the good news: 'we were reconciled to God through the death of his son, *while we were enemies*' (5.10).

If the New Community owes its existence to God's reconciliation with the enemies, then the existence of enemy lines is all but a fiction, and enmity itself is nullified. Paul's teaching here occupies the same space as Jesus's teaching, 'Love your enemy', in that both make nonsense of the idea of enemy, because authentic love hollows out hostility and turns tribalism inside out. If the Nazi sympathizer Carl Schmitt is right that the modern state is built on a distinction between friends and foes (Schmitt

2007), then Paul fundamentally rejects it. Far from banal truisms, then, the imperatives in Rom. 12.14–21 are principles necessary for the governance of not just a minor religious community but also nations and empires, if authentic peace is to be achieved. These principles form a blueprint aimed at universal transformation. This is the meaning of the New Community being transformed by the renewal of the mind (12.2). It is in enfleshing this inside-out love that the true identity and character of a New Community of Christ is embodied.

Read in this light, the instructions of 12.15–20 – all linked syntactically to 'bless the persecutors' – should not be taken as platitudes but as principles governing how the New Community should behave towards the world (Dunn 1988: 2.755). 'To rejoice with those who rejoice and to weep with those who weep, being mindful of the same thing with each other, not being mindful of the haughty but accommodating to the lowly, not repaying evil for evil but considering what is noble before all' (Rom. 12.15–17) is therefore an expression of solidarity with strangers, enemies, and all outsiders who might do us harm. But clearly Paul does not regard standards governing a community to be different from those that govern the world; tribalism is not permitted. Loving our enemies means being agents of peace 'with all people' (12.18) and turning ourselves inside out to allow the character of the New Community to spill into the world.[4] Unlike the Roman *pax* this peace is achieved not by military conquest or enslavement of the conquered but by the inclusion of Gentiles into 'All Israel' through an election of grace and by an erasure of enemy lines.

Paul provides the rationale for this inside-out love in the next two verses. We should not take vengeance into our hands because that is God's exclusive arena: 'Give space to divine wrath' (12.19). Instead, the New Community must practice inside-out love by feeding our enemies, citing Prov. 25.21–22a in support (12.20). Paul, however, replaces the last line, 'and the Lord will reward you', with a saying, 'Do not let yourself be defeated by the evil, but defeat the evil by the good' (12.21). Just as hospitality must be

---

[4] The expression 'to be at peace' (*eirēneuein*) usually refers to peace within a community in the New Testament and early Christian literature. In Mk 9.50 and 1 Thess. 5.13, the word is followed by 'among each other or yourselves', and internal peace is implied in 2 Cor. 13.11 (also *Hermas* 2.3). The only parallel to 'living in peace *with all people*' in the New Testament is found in Heb. 12.14, 'pursue (*diōkein*) peace with all', with 'all' clearly referring to outsiders who have no knowledge of the Lord. But there the apologetic intention is clear to see. This makes Paul's instructions to live peacefully with all people in Rom. 12.18 highly unusual even if it is not unique. Epictetus likewise urges that '[we] make peace with all people' as a philosophical ideal (4.5.24; cited in Dunn 1988b: 2.748).

actively pursued, feeding our enemies must likewise be practiced with no enticement of reward, because it is issued from the inner character of the New Community, and it is part of a strategy that seeks to defeat evil with inside-out love. Paul's formulation stands in stark contrast to the Roman *Pax*. He bids the New Community to resist being defeated by evil but to defeat it by genuine love – by feeding the enemies, blessing the persecutors, and crossing enemy lines to welcome them into your fold. The aim of inside-out love is not to enlarge one's territories but to give itself up in order to render the idea of territory meaningless.

The outside world imposes itself on the New Community in the form of civil authorities in 13.1–7. This controversial passage will be studied in Chapter 4; suffice to say Paul counsels no unconditional submission to the government but points to a divine ordering to which rulers and the ruled must subject themselves before God or risk God's avenging sword (13.4–5). Paul frames that discussion between inside-out love (12.9–21) and a capping statement on love (13.8–10). Paul's statement that love is the fulfilment of the law (13.8, 10) was first espoused in Gal. 5.14–15, but whereas there the focus was internal strife of a community, here the scope is universal. Loving one another (13.8a) gives way to loving 'the other' (13.8b), as exemplified by the universal commandments not to commit adultery, murder, steal, or covet (13.9), thereby making 'neighbour' into a boundary-smashing concept. Since rulers come under the same apocalyptic conditions (13.11–14), they are subject to God's eschatological wrath (12.19; 13.5), and whatever authority they possess exists only in borrowed time. If revenge is God's exclusive prerogative, the responsibility of the New Community is not to set up a competing government but to work within God's order in love. Paul resists evil regimes with an activism based not on violence or conquest but on the erasure of distinction between friend and enemy.

The Weak and the Strong (14.1–15.6)

With the start of chapter 14, Paul's didactic style changes from pithy maxims to sustained argumentation, signalling a shift from general exhortation to response to concrete issues (Dunn 1988: 2.810–12; Jewett 2006: 833–5; Longenecker 2016: 994–6). What remains unclear is the underlying problem. Because Paul identifies the 'weak' as those who eat only vegetables (14.2) and have issues with foods and drinks (14.13–23), and because Paul also identifies those who judge some days above others (14.5–6), many have suggested that the 'weak' is a code word for Jews who observe dietary laws and festival days, and the 'strong' (15.1) for Gentiles who have no such restrictions. That hypothesis would not fit a Gentile audience. Besides, 1 Corinthians amply documents that Gentile converts are perfectly capable of themselves generating such contrary responses to food and drink (1 Cor. 8.1–13; 10.23–33). Then as now, the problem could be both sociological and theological. The qualification that the vegetarians are 'weak *in faith*' suggests that not eating meat might be a matter of conscience, but given the economic conditions of the Roman congregation, material want might be an underlying issue. 'To be weak' (*asthenein*) carries a connotation of material want and destitution (BDAG 2000: 142).

Paul's ethical instructions, indeed the whole letter, draw to a close. Paul restates the Jewish character of the gospel (15.7–13) to reassert his position as the superior rabbi, the apostle to the Gentiles (15.14–21). Paul reminds his audience that he identifies Christ primarily as a 'minister (*diakonos*) of circumcision on behalf of the truth of God for the purpose of confirming the promises of the patriarchs' (15.8). In other words, Paul understands Christ strictly in the context of the covenant and its promises; only secondarily are the Gentiles included 'on behalf of mercy'. That presumably means God's mercy extends to Gentiles. Even that inclusion has a purpose – so that 'the Gentiles might glorify God' (15.9).

3

Theological Themes in Romans

The reading pursued in this volume takes Romans principally as a blueprint for reconstituting the Jewish people, the formation of Ideal Israel, under the covenant. Ideal Israel stands as a resistance to and replacement of all earthly empires but specifically the Roman Empire. Paul makes his case by using the rich resources available to him in traditional and apocalyptic Judaism and in the burgeoning Jesus-movement. In this chapter we collect theological themes scattered throughout Chapter 2 and reconsider them in the context of Paul's overall goal of ethnic construction. We might be surprised by how much Paul has added new life to old theological categories.

Good News

There is arguably no more misunderstood term in the Pauline vocabulary than 'gospel' or *euangelion*, literally 'good news'. The modern American version of 'good news' grew out of the sixteenth-century Reformers' anti-Catholic construction in that it stresses individual salvation based on personal belief in Christ. The attendant eschewal of good work rings hollow, however, because of an over-reliance on personal agency. When one's decision for or against Christ becomes the sole criterion for salvation, personal response becomes a work unto itself and the content of the good news recedes into the background. As alluded to in Chapter 1, the term 'good news' (*euangelion*) or the verb 'to proclaim the good news' (*euangelizesthai*) was typically used to announce a new ruler who promised to guide a city-state, kingdom, or even the mighty Roman Empire to new heights. It was intimately related to the emperor cult, which was as much a political tool as it was religious pageantry. The *euangelion* included announcements of extraordinary astronomical events accompanying the birth and ascension of the new ruler portending the future health and prosperity of the empire and his superhuman prowess, mighty feats, embodiment of good fortune and salvation.

Much of this political 'good news' can be documented in the famous Priene inscription (9 BCE) composed by the Asian League to heap praises on Caesar Augustus as the one chosen by Providence herself. This reads in part:

> Since Providence, which has ordered all things and is deeply interested in our life, has set in most perfect order by giving us Augustus, whom she filled with virtue that he might benefit humankind, sending him as a *saviour*, both for us and for our descendants, that he might end war and arrange all things, and since he, Caesar, by his appearance (excelled even our anticipations), surpassing all previous benefactors, and not even leaving to posterity any hope of surpassing what he has done; and since the birthday of the *god* marked for the world the beginning of *good news* through his coming.
>
> (*I. Priene* 105.32–40; trans. adapted from Price 1997: 53)

Here Augustus, whose Greek name *ho sebastos* means 'the worshipful one', is depicted as the virtuous one, a peacemaker who ends war and restores order, an august figure that surpasses all his ancestors and leaves no hope for posterity to match. He is called a 'god', a divine 'saviour' (*sōtēr*), whose birth 'marked for the world the beginning of *good news* (plural *euangelia*) through his coming'. Germanicus also called Augustus 'the true saviour and the benefactor of the entire race of men' (cited in Jewett 2006: 139). At the arrival of Augustus, therefore, universal salvation would spread like wild fires throughout the inhabited world (Deissmann 1964: 366–7; Georgi 1991: 83). 'To evangelize' (*euangelizesthai*) in that context refers to the proclamation of the emperor's coming of age, accession, conquests, exploits, victories, and similar propitious news throughout the realm (Friedrich 1964: 724–5; Longenecker 2016: 58–9).

The Priene inscription makes it clear that the old distinction between *euangelion* as the act of proclaiming good news and as content of that good news does not hold. While 'good news' refers to the propagation of that news as it reverberates from land to land, the context quite clearly describes what that good news is all about: namely, a divine saviour who even at birth is destined to lead the empire to greater heights and longer-lasting peace unattained either before or after. It includes in itself both the act of proclamation and the content of that proclamation.

Paul's use of *euangelion* in Romans follows the same convention. He pins his much-contested title apostle on the principal task for which he is called: proclaiming 'the good news of God' (1.1), but he immediately clarifies what the good news consists of: 'that was promised beforehand through his prophets in holy scriptures concerning his son who came out of the seed of David according to the flesh, designated Son of God in power according to the spirit of holiness by resurrection from the dead, Jesus Christ our Lord' (1.2–4). In claiming Jesus to be an integral part of such 'good news', Paul counters the Roman political-theological propaganda that the emperor is the 'saviour' of the world with a Jesus who by means of his resurrection from the dead has been made the cosmic Son of God. The 'Son of God' was itself a political-theological title favoured by imperial propaganda, with the emperor frequently depicted in coins and public inscriptions as the *divi filius*. The irony of Paul's claim could not have escaped his Roman readers: this messianic-kingly figure turns out to be a political criminal executed at the hands of the same imperial masters over whom Jesus now stands as the true divine ruler. The defeated is now been made victor. The reference to the resurrection is a not-so-veiled interjection of the cross, symbol of Roman imperial violence and political suppression, into Jesus's messianic claim.

References to traditional Jewish political-theological terms make Paul's 'good news' not only cosmic but Jewish. By linking it to ancient prophecies long encoded in the holy scriptures, Paul claims the good news of God has been predestined from the beginning, 'promised beforehand' to prophets – qua *Jewish* prophets – of old, but its true intent and fulfilment are revealed only now, in the fullness of time. The Jewish character of the good news is further reinforced by the incarnation, not merely in Jesus's becoming a human being but in his coming as 'the seed of David according to the flesh'.

The Jewish character makes Paul's anti-imperial rhetoric stronger, not weaker, for it forces us to hear the good news on the human and political plane instead of consigning it to some abstract universalist realm. In contradistinction from the imperial claims that Caesar is lord and saviour, the gospel of the crucified Jesus is 'the power of God for the purpose of salvation to everyone who believe…' (1.16), Paul announces in his thesis statement for Romans. 'By implication, … if such salvation comes as a result of the gospel that Paul proclaims about Christ crucified and resurrected, then salvation must not be present in the accoutrements of Roman rule that filled the city to which this letter was addressed' (Jewett 2006: 139).

Justice/Righteousness of God

Since the Reformation, there has been endless discussion on the meaning of 'righteousness' or 'justice' (*dikaiosynē*) in Romans. Should it mean a pronouncement of innocence despite continual moral imperfection, or should it refer to moral transformation that makes one righteous? While that debate lingers at the level of the individual, we have come to appreciate a Paul who is immersed in the political-theological struggles of his days. This is evident the first time Paul introduces the term, in its full expression 'justice or righteousness of God', to his Roman audience in his thesis statement:

> For I am not ashamed of the good news, for it is the power of God for salvation to everyone who has faith, to the Jew first but also the Greek. For the *justice/ righteousness of God* is revealed in it from faith to faith, as it is written, 'The righteous by faith will live'.

> (1.16–17)

The good news, whose political-theological character has just been discussed above, is here called 'power of God for salvation'. This points to the extraordinary capacity of God to author such mighty acts as the resurrection that installs Christ as the cosmic Son of God, the divinely appointed saviour who supersedes and eclipses all self-appointed saviours (1.3). The good news is also the vehicle by or in which the righteousness of God is revealed. The short prepositional phrase 'in it' (1.17) could be taken in the locative sense indicating the good news is where the righteousness of God is found. Or it is used instrumentally, with the good news being the means by which the righteousness of God is revealed. Either way, if the good news is the medium through which God reveals to humanity and it is characterized as power, righteousness of God likewise points to divine initiative. God is the author of both power and righteousness. Moreover, the justice of God is here introduced as a present, ongoing revelation. Similarly in 3.21, 'the justice of God has come to be disclosed (Greek perfect tense)' as attested by scripture.

While it is true that in Romans justice of God is delimited by 'redemption that is in Christ Jesus' (Dunn 1988a: 1.169), 'redemption' here must be understood in a broader, political sense. Righteousness of God in biblical literature is linked to the Davidic king-messiah who will 'execute justice and righteousness in the land. In his days Judah will be saved and Israel will live in safety. And this is the name by which he will be called: "The LORD is our righteousness"' (Jer. 23.5–6 NRSV). The usage of the phrase in Qumran is also tied to the redemption of a people: 'To you does righteousness belong, and blessing belongs to your name for ever. [Act according] to your righteousness and redeem [your servant] and may the wicked come to an end' (1QH 4, cited in Jewett 2006: 142; also 1QM 4.6). Paul likewise has in mind the redemption of the people. The justice of God is disclosed 'through the faithfulness of Jesus Christ… for all who believe, for there is no distinction' (Rom. 3.22). The distinction being erased is explicitly stated as between Jews and Gentiles, but for his audience, the stress lies entirely with the Gentiles. By placing the Gentiles on the same plane as the Jews, Paul makes it possible for Gentiles 'to become right' with God, alongside Jews, through the same 'free offer of his grace through the redemption that is in Christ Jesus' (3.24). It has been suggested that Paul's understanding of God's justice should be interpreted in terms of the new creation (2 Cor. 5.17; Käsemann 1969b). But Paul's eager expectation is realized only with the restoration of Israel and the fulfilment of the covenant in the end time (Wright 2013). It is just that for Paul the boundaries of Ideal Israel have been extended outwards to encompass the 'fullness of Gentiles' (Rom. 11.25), so they too might join the Jews in receiving the justice of God.

'Righteousness' (*dikaiosynē*) appears in Romans thirty-four times, by far the most among New Testament books, but the full expression 'righteousness of God' appears only eight times, all but two of which appear in the first three chapters of Romans, with the last two appearing in 10.3. The expression is a common one in the biblical text, with the highest concentration found in the Psalms and in Deutero-Isaiah. In Ps. 36.5–6, the psalmist sings praises to the LORD:

> Your *covenant love*, O LORD, extends to the heavens,
>   your *faithfulness* to the clouds.
>   Your *righteousness* is like the mighty mountains,
>   your *judgements* are like the great deep;
>   you save humans and animals alike, O LORD.
>   (NRSV modified, emphasis added)

Here God's righteousness is used in conjunction with steadfast love or covenant love (*ḥesed*), faithfulness, and judgement. A similar set of terms are also clustered in Ps. 40.9–10, where in the Greek translation (LXX 39.10–11) they are explicitly linked up with many of Paul's favourite terms:

I *preached* (*euēngelisamēn*) *righteousness* (*dikaiosynēn*) in the great
congregation (*ekklēsia*)
　　Lo, I will not hold back my lips,
　　LORD, [as] you know
Your *righteousness* I have not hidden in my heart
　　I have said your *truth* and *salvation*;
I have not concealed your *mercy* and your *truth*
　　from the great *congregation*.

Most informative for our purpose is perhaps Ps. 103.17–18, in which
these attributes of God are placed in the context of the covenant and its
commandments:

But the *steadfast love* of the LORD is from everlasting to everlasting
　　on those who fear him,
　　and his *righteousness* to children's children,
to those who keep his *covenant*
　　and remember to do his *commandments*.

(NRSV, emphasis added)

From these and other examples (Pss. 88.11–12; 98.2–3; 111.3–4; 119.40–41;
143.1, 11–12; 145.7), it seems most natural to understand the righteousness
of God in the context of the covenant. While other qualities of God such
as faithfulness and covenant love are often mentioned with the covenant,
righteousness is explicitly stressed as the essential condition for and
character of the covenant in Isa. 42.6:

I am the LORD, I have called you in *righteousness*,
　　I have taken you by the hand and kept you;
I have given you as a *covenant* to the people,
　　a light to the nations.

(NRSV, emphasis added)

A covenantal approach to the righteousness of God would make perfect
sense with how the term is used in the chapters on Abraham and Christ
the Second Adam (Rom. 4–5). Citing Gen. 15.6, 'Abraham had faith in God
and it was reckoned to him unto righteousness' (Rom. 4.3), Paul argues
that the covenant God established with the father of all Jews was possible
because Abraham did not do anything to earn his status (4.5-6). The odd
phrase 'it was reckoned to him unto righteousness', paraphrased (4.6, 9) or
quoted verbatim (4.22), 'has to do with ascription of status, in the instance
of Abraham, declaring someone to be something he was not' (Jewett, 314,
citing Wis. 3.17). So it is Paul's understanding that Abraham's trust makes it

possible for God to declare him righteous even though he was not in reality. The relationship between faith and righteousness is so complete that Paul could say, '[Abraham's] faith is reckoned as righteousness' (4.5, 9). Nowhere does Paul speak of faith as an accomplishment that can earns righteousness, which remains a free gift (5.17, 21). So faith here really means surrendering one's prerogatives (see below Faith/Belief/Trust) as a precondition for ratification of the covenant (4.11).

Dikaiosynē as covenantal righteousness is the only way to understand why 'Gentiles who did not pursue righteousness received righteousness' (9.30). They are 'righteous' in that they have been incorporated into the covenant, even though they never looked to be a part of the covenantal people. This is also confirmed by Paul's use of the verb 'to make righteous' or 'to justify' (*dikaioun*) throughout Romans. In the majority of cases, it is used in the passive voice to imply divine agency (2.13; 3.20, 24, 28; 4.2; 5.1, 9, etc.) or directly in the active voice with God as the subject (3.26, 30; 4.5; 8.30, 33). But it is especially in the context of the Abrahamic covenant where Paul tips his hand. Abraham would have a basis for pride if he 'had been made righteous on the basis of works' (4.2), but because he surrendered himself ('had faith') to God who makes the impious righteous – that is, to make outsiders into a covenantal people – he was counted as 'righteous', which is to say he has been granted a covenant with God (4.5).

Given this covenantal connection, to say righteousness means declaration of unearned innocence is accurate but inadequate. Insofar as divine election means God freely '[makes] the impious righteous' (4.5), the sinners become righteous because God says so. But righteousness is also a status within a covenant that implies obligations, obligations that are both personal and communal, individual and corporate. After all, the object of the covenant, first and foremost, is the formation of a people of God. The pronouncement of innocence, therefore, includes a responsibility to become innocent. This is where the indicative calls forth an imperative: If you are righteous, make yourself righteous! Become who you are! This notion of obligation is precisely what Paul tries to convey with the religio-mythological language of power and dominance in chapter 6: 'Do not present your members as weapons of wickedness for Sin, but present yourselves to God, as if you are alive from dead, and your members as weapons of righteousness to God' (6.13, but also 16 & 18).

To think merely in terms of innocence and morality, however, can lure us into the modern trap of individualism. Paul's world was informed by covenant, election, and peoplehood. In Pss. 36.6; 103.18, covenantal righteousness is coordinated with commandments and judgement. In Isa. 58.2, judgement is used as a synonym for righteousness:

> Yet day after day they seek me
>> and delight to know my ways,
> as if they were a nation that practiced *righteousness*
>> and did not forsake the ordinance of their God;
> they ask of me *righteous judgements,*
>> they delight to draw near to God.

(NRSV, emphasis added)

'Righteous judgements' here carry no negative connotation. To an oppressed people victimized by unjust laws, 'righteous judgement' is tantamount to salvation. In fact, righteousness is so bound up with God's saving act that it is synonymous with 'salvation' of the people of God (Isa. 51.5; cf. also Isa. 41.2; 45.8).

Faith/Belief/Trust

'Faith in Jesus or Jesus Christ' is such a stock phrase in modern Protestantism that we might be surprised to learn that it appears only twice in the *New Revised Standard Version* translation of Romans (3.22 & 26), even though the word 'faith' (*pistis*) appears a total of thirty-five times in the letter. The underlying phrase *pistis Iēsou Christou* is capable of meaning 'faith *in* Jesus Christ', taking Jesus Christ as the object of faith; or 'the faithfulness *of* Jesus Christ', taking faithfulness to be the quality that describes Christ's self-sacrifice. The NRSV Rom. 3.22 takes Jesus Christ to be the object of faith, but that would refer to the believer's faith in Christ twice: 'the righteousness of God [came] through *faith in Jesus Christ* for all who *believe*'. The context favours the second option. Starting with 3.21, the stress is on *God's justice*, promised long ago in the scriptures and being revealed now. True justice is established entirely through God's initiative. Taking *pistis Iēsou Christou* as 'faith *in* Jesus Christ' would make it sound as if the establishment of the justice of God depended on human faith in Christ. A better translation might therefore read: 'the justice of God [came] through the *faithfulness of Jesus Christ* for all who believe', that is, for all who trust Paul's message that God has accomplished through the death and resurrection of Christ. *Pistis* can mean 'trustworthiness or faithfulness' as well as 'faith', and in 3.22, it refers to what Christ has faithfully fulfilled God's plan of salvation through his death and resurrection. A similar expression found in the same context should be translated the same way: God tolerates transgressions to demonstrate that

God is just and justifies 'one who is issued from the faithfulness of Jesus' (*ton ek pisteōs Iēsou*, 3.26). The awkward phrase is a shorthand for 'follower of Jesus', a Gentile in the case of Romans who becomes the beneficiary of Christ's faithfulness. If we discount these two verses, 'faith in Jesus' is actually missing from Paul's theological vocabulary in Romans.

When we turn to the verb *pisteuein* ('to believe, to have faith, to trust'), the results are even more disappointing. Of the twenty-one times it appears in Romans, six times Paul uses it without an object, probably intending it as a short hand for follower (1.16; 3.22; 4.11; 10.4; 13.11; 15.13). Eight times the object of belief is either a message like Paul's good news (10.9, 10, 14 [2x], 16), a teaching such as our future resurrection (6.8) or that all foods are permissible (14.2), or the oracles of God (3.2). Five times Paul speaks of believing a person, all occurring in chapter 4, in the context of discussing Abraham's faith in God or in God's word or action (4.3, 5, 17, 18, 24). This is also where *pisteuein* is used without an object (4.11), but context makes it clear that it refers to the faith that Abraham exemplifies, that is, to believe in God's faithfulness. The last two uses of the verb come in the form of 'to believe in it/him' (9.33; 10.11). The phrase is a citation from Isaiah (Rom. 9.33), but it is clear in 10.11 that 'it' refers to Paul's message 'that God raised [Christ] from the dead' (10.9). Nowhere in Romans does Paul say 'believe Christ' or 'believe in Christ' in a way that is comparable to his description of Abraham as believing God or believing in God. Faith for Paul centres not so much on one's personal decision for or against Christ but on believing the good news that God has reconciled the Gentiles – while they were still enemies who should have been merited no consideration – through the death and resurrection of Christ, now installed as the cosmic Son of the living God.

Paul does not reject personal volition or decision, but for him the good news begins and ends with what God has wrought through Jesus *and* his *faithfulness* (*pistis*) in fulfilling God's plan, in his death and resurrection. The initiative lies entirely with God through the self-sacrificial faithfulness of Christ; followers could do no more than simply 'to believe' Paul's message. In that regard, 'to believe' comes close to 'to obey or to surrender'.

But surrender to what or to whom? Paul's conception of faith is not merely a general advice for personal obedience to God but a call to submit to the divine initiative of offering membership to the covenant first inaugurated with Abraham and confirmed through the patriarchs. In that the covenant was first established out of election and maintained by God's covenantal faithfulness, and in that it was received by faith by Abraham while he was still 'impious', the only way to enter the covenant is to emulate the patriarch's example, to receive the free offer by faith. This was how the Jews became a covenantal people, and it is the exact same way in which Gentiles, Paul's intended audience of Romans, enter into a covenant heretofore closed to them – not because anyone, Jew or Gentile, has done anything to merit inclusion but because of divine election. The covenant has always been about faith, not works.

Works of the Law

Modern scholarship has thankfully moved passed the Reformation-era argument that identified the expression 'works of the law' with the Jewish law. According to that standard Protestant interpretation, Paul the Christian rejected the law and the works-righteousness of Judaism, for reasons never explained with any satisfaction, and replaced it with Christ's gospel of grace. Paul's fellow-Jews, so goes the argument, thought they could be 'saved' only if they kept all the commandments. After a lifetime of striving and failing to fulfil the law, Paul abandoned hope in earning his way into God's good grace. Because no one could ever hope to fulfil the whole law, Christ makes it possible to rely solely on God's grace. We are all judged, therefore, not by our moral failings but on the basis of faith alone. 'Christ is the end – termination – of the law', so Rom. 10.4 was translated to reflect this position. It took centuries for Protestants to reject this anti-Jewish interpretation.

Krister Stendahl first raised doubts about this characterization of Paul, who in fact had a rather robust image of himself and his Jewish tradition (2 Cor. 11.22; Gal. 1.13–14; Phil. 3.4–6; Stendahl 1976). This is particularly true with his letter to the Romans, in which he revels in his Jewish identity and attendant prerogatives (Rom. 9.1–5). He unambiguously calls the law and the commandments 'holy and just and good' (7.12). And he devotes considerable effort to expounding on rewards and punishment for good and evil deeds (2.6–11), a positive evaluation of circumcision (2.25–27), and meaning of a true Jew (2.28–29). None of these statements could have been uttered by someone having turned his back on his ancestral traditions.

The final blow to the old Protestant position was dealt by E. P. Sanders's 1977 book *Paul and Palestinian Judaism* (Sanders 1977). In it Sanders concludes that Paul's Jewish contemporaries all subscribed to divine election which brought about the covenant and none believed that one could earn one's way into the covenant by following the Mosaic Law. They nevertheless followed all the commandments as part of their covenantal obligations. Failure to do so could jeopardize one's standings in the covenant, but the law also provides means of atonement. The role the law plays within the covenant Sanders dubs 'covenantal nomism'. In sum, first-century Judaism was not a legalistic religion but one patterned by a healthy view of election. This picture is consistent with the Paul of Romans, who defends the law, eschews boasting, and champions divine election.

These insights brought about a revolution to our reading of Paul, but they also opened up new, enduring questions. First and foremost, if there was no substantial difference between first-century Judaism and the Jesus-movement in their views of the law and election, what was so unique about Paul's vision? Indeed, what was Paul's objection to other forms of Judaism? Sanders's own answer is that to Paul, Judaism was simply not Christianity. Only after Paul became a follower of Christ did he begin to formulate a question to fit his answer. That ingenious answer finds little support today partly because Sanders himself might not have realized how radical his own thesis was. He was still operating under the unexamined assumption that Judaism and Pauline Christianity represented mutually exclusive movements. Paul would not share that perspective. Instead, he thought of himself as a reformer within his ancestral tradition attempting to open up the covenantal boundaries to include Gentiles who had been excluded from the covenant up till now. Paul never left Judaism at all but in light of his experience of the resurrected Christ now realized the long-awaited eschatological upheaval that would sweep aside all earthly powers in favour of the peaceable kingdom was about to take place. The salvation of the world would begin with calling together a community out of Jews and Gentiles, a remnant that would sow the seed of reform within Judaism and, through Judaism, the world. It is pointless to ask why Paul left behind Judaism for a new religion when he never did.

Paul, however, does rail against the 'works of the law' (3.20, 27, 28) or simply 'works' (4.2, 6; 9.12, 32; 11.6) and places them in opposition to faith. The expression came in prominence when Paul confronted the Galatians – Gentiles all – who were being seduced to go through circumcision (Gal. 2.16 [3x]; 3.2, 10). That is surely one of the referents in Romans as well, especially in chapter 4 where Abraham's circumcision is described as a 'seal of justice' that he received while still uncircumcised, 'in order that he would become the father of all who have faith through their foreskin' (4.11). God had declared covenantal righteousness on Abraham when he trusted God; circumcision came later as a sign but did not and indeed could not alter the substance of the covenant. It is in this specific sense related to the circumcision that Abraham is not 'justified by works' (4.2). The same idea is repeated four verses later (4.6).

But in Romans, Paul does not dismiss circumcision categorically. Compared to his blanket denunciation of circumcision in Galatians (Gal. 5.2–3), his discussion in Rom. 2.25–29 is surprisingly positive (for longer discussion, see Wan 2009: 151–3). Critics of Judaism had singled out circumcision as proof of Jewish perverse intransigence to assimilating to Greek culture. That elevated it to the status of an ethnic marker (Cohen 1999: 109–39, especially 135–9; Dunn, *Romans,* 1.159; Keener, *Romans,* 56). Paul's Jewish contemporaries Josephus and Philo were loath to abandon circumcision even as they struggled to answer their detractors. Philo interpreted it allegorically as excising fleshly passions but defended the rite itself for its cultural significance to Jewish tradition (Hecht 1984; Barclay 1998). By contrast Paul replaces circumcision as an ethnic marker with what it signifies, 'doing the law'. The replacement is so thorough that it can be reversed allegorically: 'If you are a transgressor of the law, your circumcision becomes your foreskin', and anyone who keeps the requirements of the law can turn his foreskin into circumcision (Rom. 2.25–26).

The theme of doing what the law requires runs through the whole of 1.18–2.29, thus linking together two types of judgement. The theme of 'practicing' wickedness unites those who know God's law but 'practice' vices (mentioned twice in 1.32) and those who pass judgement on others but 'practice' the same thing themselves (2.1, 3). The same goes with those who 'do' what should not be done (1.28, 32) and those who judge others but do the very same thing themselves (2.3). On the flip side, circumcision is beneficial only if one keeps the righteous deeds of the law. If one judges on the basis of physical circumcision (2.1–3), then those who remain uncircumcised but keep the law will judge those who have the mark of circumcision but transgress the law (2.27). All this is to demonstrate God's impartiality (Bassler 1982: 131–3).

Paul's distinction between circumcision and the requirements of the law should be ample proof that he is not equating works of the law to the law itself and he most certainly is not rejecting the Torah. But if that is the case, what are his problems with 'works of the law'? The answer can be found in the conclusion of his discussion on the inclusion of Gentiles into Ideal Israel (3.27–31). As discussed in Chapter 2, Paul rejects legalism, but legalism as practiced by Gentile converts who, in their competition with erstwhile Jewish leaders returning to Rome after their exile, glory in their circumcision, their supercilious adherence to the law, their credentials. Against them, Paul expands 'works of the law' to include all kinds of human accomplishments that promote boasting (3.27). The law is holy and good and it must be fulfilled and its commandments followed, but one does so as a grateful recipient of divine grace in the inclusion of Gentiles, heretofore enemies of God. The law is fulfilled not by stressing one's accomplishments ('law of works', 3.28) but by surrendering oneself to God's faithfulness ('law of faith', 3.27).

The criticism against legalism is so broadened that it is later applied also to the election of Jacob and Esau. Rebecca was simply informed that between his two sons 'the elder shall serve the younger' even before they were born, before they had a chance to accrue any accomplishments, in order to demonstrate that election comes not by works by the one who calls the people into a covenantal relationship (9.11–12). The same could be said of the contrast between the Gentiles not striving but attaining righteousness and Israel striving and not attaining (9.30–31). The reason? 'Because it is not by faith but as by works' (9.32). We need to be careful here and not to construe Paul's rhetoric as a rejection of Israel. The object of the whole of chapters 9–11 is to inform his *Gentile* audience why Israel is momentarily left out of the covenant (11.13). The focus is on the Gentiles' self-understanding *vis-à-vis* the position of Physical Israel. In that respect, Paul reminds his audience once again that they owe their current position not to anything they have done but on divine initiative, to which the only proper response is by faith or submission (11.6).

Paul's objection to the 'works of the law' belongs to the same type of prophetic self-criticism as found in Isaiah 58. The people complain that they have done everything correctly yet God still abandons them:

Why do we fast, but you do not see?
  Why humble ourselves, but you do not notice?

(Isa. 58.3)

Fasting is beneficial only if they have 'done righteousness' (Isa. 58.2), the prophet chides before continuing:

Is not this the fast that I choose:
  to loose the bonds of injustice,
  to undo the thongs of the yoke,
to let the oppressed go free,
  and to break every yoke?
Is it not to share your bread with the hungry,
  and bring the homeless poor into your house;

> when you see the naked, to cover them,
>   and not to hide yourself from your own kin?

(Isa. 58.6–7)

If only the people pursue God's righteousness by adhering not to the external trappings of their religiosity but to the demands they signify, 'then you shall call, and the LORD will answer' (Isa. 58.9). Paul makes the same hermeneutical move in Romans: to reject the external in favour of the internal. The success of the Gentile mission shows that God has now made the covenant available to outsiders, if only they, like Abraham, surrender to God without relying on their own merits and accomplishments. All the external trappings are mere 'works of the law' and can in no way invalidate the original promise.

Eschatology

From the moment he invokes the resurrection of Christ in the prescript (Rom. 1.4), Paul sets a course that culminates in the salvation of 'all Israel' in the end time (11.26). The whole of Romans is cast within an apocalyptic framework. Unlike his other letters, however, Paul's exposition of the apocalyptic theme is triggered neither by pastoral issues, as in 1 Thessalonians, nor by polemics, as is the case in 1 Corinthians, but by his political-theological vision. The resurrection demonstrates to him that God's fulfilment of the covenantal promises made to the people of God is near its completion, and the final step of including heretofore enemies, Gentiles, is being taken.

For their part, Gentiles should be grateful for the grace that has been shown to them, but more importantly, they need to be vigilant in holding on to what they have been given till the end, lest they be swept up by the cataclysmic wrath that is about to be unleashed. 'Wrath' (*orgē*) belongs to Paul's special eschatological vocabulary, especially in Romans. In his fifteen uses of the word, twelve appear in Romans alone (1.18; 2.5 [2x], 8; 3.5; 4.15; 5.9; 9.22 [2x]; 12.19; 13.4, 5) and the other three appear in 1 Thessalonians (1.10; 2.16; 5.9). In all fifteen cases, God is the author of wrath in an apocalyptic context, which is either stated explicitly (e.g. 2.5, 8; 5.9; 9.22; cf. 1 Thess. 1.10; 5.9) or implied (e.g. 12.19; 13.4, 5; cf. 1 Thess. 2.16). It is an anthropomorphism that describes God's action using a human analogue (Longenecker 2016: 201–2), but it describes not much the emotion as the action of God, as is indicated by the word's frequent association with the notion of justice (Dunn 1998: 1.54–55). Wrath will be unleashed in the end time in punishment for sin, disobedience to truth, and other wickedness (2.5, 8), whereas those who wait upon God will be saved from the coming onslaught (5.9). To be rescued from the impending unleashing of God's wrath was likely a central tenet of Paul's preaching, as attested in 1 Thess. 1.10. Gentile converts in the Pauline communities are said to be eagerly awaiting the Son from heaven to rescue them from the imminent wrath of God.

Those who are threatened by the impending wrath await rescue, as can be documented by Paul's use of *sōzein* 'to save' (Rom. 5.9–10 [2x]; 8.24; 9.27; 10.9; 10.13; 11.14, 26). In all eight cases, the verb is used in the future tense; the only exception is 8.24, where the past tense is used from the perspective of the future. In all but one, the verb is used in Paul's customary divine passive to point to God as the ultimate author of salvation. The only time Paul says 'I will save' (11.14), he uses it to stress his willingness to take part in a divine plan to save his kinsfolk regardless of personal cost to himself. The final time the verb appears in Romans, 'thus all Israel *will be saved*' (11.26), represents the goal towards which Paul's saving language is directed. The eschatological character of the verb *sōzein* is unmistakable, but it is a natural consequence of justification. When Paul is drawing out the implications of atonement, he explicitly ties it to justification and what that means for salvation in the end time: 'If we have been *justified* now by his blood, how much more will we be *saved* from the wrath! For if while we were enemies we were reconciled to God through the death of his son, how much more will we, being reconciled, be *saved* by his life!' (5.9–10). The two uses of *sōzein* in this passage anticipate the new creation when we are saved in hope (8.24), but they also look forward to the future salvation of 'all Israel', which will be the feature event that anchors the end time (9.27; 10.9, 13; 11.14, 26).

Most revealing about Paul's eschatology are the passages that refer to the wrath of God in the present (1.18; 4.15; 9.22). The present manifestation of wrath is not final but serves as a warning and foretaste for the end time: 'If God who wishes to demonstrate his wrath and to make known his power, endured with much patience vessels of wrath being prepared for destruction' (9.22). The present does not so much anticipate the future as it is being evaluated from the viewpoint of the end time. The future breaks into the present in the form of the ongoing struggle between Old Adam's reign and New Adam's. As discussed in Chapter 2, the simultaneous existence of the two reigns is possible because New Adam has been appointed as a result of the resurrection, while Old Adam continues to exert his deleterious influence on his subjects in the mean time. The future has broken into the present because an eschatological event, Christ's resurrection, has taken place in real time and space. By presenting Christ as New Adam, Paul makes it clear the end will be just like the beginning. Adam belongs to the old creation, but the New Adam belongs to the new creation in which all will be renewed and nothing will be subjected to death and decay. That the end time is a restoration of the bounty of the earth is a rich theme amply attested in the Prophets. New heavens and new earth will be created, new houses and bountiful vineyards will be the rule, Jerusalem will be rebuilt, and the covenant renewed (Isa. 65.17–25). In the wild, fish will be plentiful and all kinds of trees will grow to provide for food (Ezek. 47.9–12). Most important, death will be no more, and the terrible curse that came into the world as a result of the fall will be reversed (Isa. 25.6–8). All these themes are neatly summarized in Amos's vision:

> The time is surely coming, says the LORD,
>> when the one who plows shall overtake the one who reaps,
>> and the treader of grapes the one who sows the seed;
>> the mountains shall drip sweet wine,
>> and all the hills shall flow with it.
> I will restore the fortunes of my people Israel,
>> and they shall rebuild the ruined cities and inhabit them;
>> they shall plant vineyards and drink their wine,
>> and they shall make gardens and eat their fruit.
> I will plant them upon their land,
>> and they shall never again be plucked up
>> out of the land that I have given them,
> says the LORD your God.
>
> (Amos 9.13–15)

Collection for the Poor among the Saints

Towards the end of Romans and in the midst of proposing a visit to Rome so they could support his Spanish mission, he lets on that while the letter he is composing will be sent via a carrier westward from Corinth, where he is staying as Gaius's guest (16.23), he is about to set sail eastward to deliver a sum of money he has collected from the Gentiles to the congregation in Jerusalem:

> Now I go to Jerusalem ministering to the saints, for Macedonia and Achaia were pleased to put together a fellowship for the poor of the saints in Jerusalem. For they were pleased [to do it] and are their debtors, for if the

Gentiles shared in their spiritual things, they owe [it to them] to serve them in their fleshly things.

(15.25–27)

That Paul would share his travelogue with his audience is not surprising; it is a regular feature of his letters. But why go into such details about a project already completed when he is trying to raise funds? Is it so straightforward as just to demonstrate his track record on managing funds?

The collection was first broached at the Jerusalem meeting between the 'pillars' and Paul's entourage (Gal. 2.1–10). Towards the end of a carefully worded report, Paul tells his Galatian audience that the Jerusalem leaders asked them to do one thing: ' … that we remember the poor, which very same thing I was eager to do' (Gal. 2.10). Thereafter Paul expended great energy and political capitals completing the project. He had solicited funds from the congregations in Galatia (1 Cor. 16.1), which would explain why he could simply mention the collection to the Galatians without introduction. He approached the congregations in Macedonia (Rom. 15.26; 2 Cor. 8.1; 9.2), where the congregations of Thessalonica and Philippi are located. He, of course, also persuaded the Corinthians to contribute to the collection, but that was also where he encountered the greatest resistance.

Most of the congregations most likely took part in the project willingly, since we can detect no voiced objections from them. With Corinth, however, while some clearly heeded Paul's call, there must have been significant opposition as well if we judge by Paul's polemics. In spite of writing two letters to urge the Corinthians to ready their contribution (2 Corinthians 8–9), not to mention an earlier reminder (1 Cor. 16.1–4), and in spite of despatching two of his trusty duties, Timothy and Titus, to coordinate the effort (2 Cor. 1.19; 8.23), some Corinthians were deeply suspicious that Paul and his colleagues were defrauding them. Paul complains bitterly that some characterize him as 'crafty' while insinuating that Titus and others took advantage of them (2 Cor. 12.16–18).

The root cause could be traced to Paul's refusal to be supported financially by the Corinthians (1 Cor. 9.6–7, 12–18; 2 Cor. 11.7–9), which was a refusal of their patronage. He was not adverse to patronage as such, because he did take advantage of the social system. He did it to maintain his independence from the Corinthians (1 Cor. 9.1), because he did receive supports from the Macedonians and others *while* he was in Corinth (2 Cor. 11.8–9)! Herein lies the rub. In the eyes of the Corinthians, Paul lords over them by denying their patronage but asks them for money nonetheless. What the right hand refuses, the left hand makes up with some story about a collection. That suspicion was at least one of the causes for the notorious factionalism among the Corinthian congregations (1 Cor. 1.10–17). The Corinthian crisis deteriorated to such a degree that Paul felt compelled to threaten the troublemakers with a 'third visit' and harsh punishments (2 Cor. 12.14; 13.1–2).

By the time Paul settled down to write Romans, he and his critics evidently had reached a truce. Paul wrote Romans under the patronage of Gaius (Rom. 16.23), one of Paul's first converts (1 Cor. 1.14) and likely one of the leaders in the Corinthians congregations. The congregations must have agreed eventually to take part in the collection, as Paul reports that 'Macedonia and Achaia' contributed to the effort (Rom. 15.26), Corinth being the major city in the Roman province of Achaia. But even here, Paul could not resist a jab. In listing Macedonia and Achaia in that order, Paul hints that he thought the Macedonian partnership was more significant, perhaps mirroring the larger share they contributed, perhaps reflecting the year of rancour over the issue (for chronicle of the collection, see Wan 2000a: 193–6; Wan 2000b: 99–124).

By now, Paul deems the project significant enough that he decides to hand-deliver to Jerusalem. That was not the case at first. In the earlier letter of 1 Corinthians, he introduces the topic with no introduction: 'Concerning the collection for the saints' (1 Cor. 16.1). 'Concerning… ' is a favourite formula of Paul's to introduce his answers to questions previously raised by his audience (cf. 1 Thess. 4.9; 5.1; 1 Cor. 7.1; 12.1, etc.). The collection was no doubt one of the questions brought to Paul by 'Chloe's people' (1 Cor. 1.11), which might be clue that trouble was already brewing. At that time, Paul was noncommittal about delivering the collection to its destination personally. He said, instead: 'I will send whomever you approve, with letters, to take your gift to Jerusalem, but if it is worthwhile that I go as well, they will accompany me' (1 Cor. 16.3–4). By the time he brought the project to a successful completion, however, he thought it important to travel to Jerusalem with the collection, so much so he is willing even to delay a long-planned mission to the ends of the earth. In the intervening time, Paul must have seen the potentials of the collection for bringing the Gentiles and Jews together.

After he shares with his Roman audience his imminent travel to Jerusalem, Paul springs a surprise on them when he asks them to join him in prayer. He asks them to pray for two things: 'that I be *rescued from the unbelievers in Judea* and my *ministry for Jerusalem* [that is, the collection] *be well received* by the saints, and that when I come to you in joy I be refreshed in your company' (Rom. 15.31–32). What could 'rescued from the unbelievers in

Judea' mean? The verb 'rescue' (*rhyesthai*) is consistently used by Paul to mean deliverance from physical danger (7.24; 11.26; 2 Cor. 1.10 [3x]; 1 Thess. 1.10; Dunn 1988b: 878). The verb *apeithein* ('to disobey, disbelieve') is found only in Romans among Paul's letters, and it consistently implies serious deviation from knowledge or lesson that could save the wayward. While the verb can be applied equally to Jews (10.21; 11.31) and Gentiles (2.8; 11.30), the qualification 'in Judea' leaves no doubt that Paul fears the Judeans who do not acknowledge Jesus as messiah are lying in wait for him in Jerusalem to inflict physical harm. Luke reports that this in fact happened, if his account is to be trusted (Acts 21.27–36). Moreover, the prayer for deliverance from the 'unbelievers' and acceptance of the collection are structured as one single request, both governed by the same *hina* ('that or in order that'). The NRSV and most modern translations unwittingly obscure this by separating the two into unrelated requests, when Paul regards them as two sides of the same coin. In Paul's mind, reception of the collection by the saints could trigger a threat of physical harm from 'unbelievers in Judea.'

The reason is likely a backlash against Paul's inclusion of Gentiles in his universal vision of the covenantal people by those who are against expanding the Jewish borders (Wan 2000a: 209–10). While universalism has always been a part of Jewish thoughts, especially among the prophets, it was understood that Gentiles could enter the covenant only after they erase their Gentile identity by becoming thoroughly Jewish. That was why the circumcision was so elevated: it signifies someone's willingness to leave behind his former life to embrace the living God, to enter into a covenantal relationship with God and with his fellow-Jews. Paul's vision threatens that project not by denouncing this form of universalism but by replacing it with an even more radical one. Paul promises Gentiles that they could remain as they are – provided they accept the offer through faithful obedience. In a few decades, history would prove Paul's universalism unsustainable; emerging normative Judaism judged it out of bounds and heretical. Nevertheless, Paul the reluctant separatist did manage to plant a seed that would flower into its own religious movement.

4

Church and State: Romans 13.1–7

In defence of his administration's 2018 policy to separate children from their parents seeking asylum at the US borders, attorney general Jeff Sessions offered this justification: 'I would cite you to the Apostle Paul and his clear and wise command in Romans 13, to obey the laws of the government because God has ordained them for the purpose of order. Orderly and lawful processes are good in themselves and protect the weak and lawful'. White House press secretary Sarah Huckabee Sanders alluded to the same passage in support: 'I can say that it is very biblical to enforce the law. That is actually repeated a number of times throughout the Bible. It's a moral policy to follow and enforce the law' (Long 2018). Sessions and Sanders had been anticipated by American Vice-President Mike Pence, who a year earlier used Paul to exhort graduates of the US Naval Academy to follow their commanders: 'Follow the chain of command without exception. *Submit yourselves,* as the saying goes, *to the authorities that have been placed above you.* Trust your superiors, trust your orders, and you'll serve and led well' (Pence 2017, emphasis added). The full text of Rom. 13.1–7 reads:

> Let every person be subject to the governing authorities; for there is no authority except from God, and those authorities that exist have been instituted by God. Therefore whoever resists authority resists what God has appointed, and those who resist will incur judgement. For rulers are not a terror to good conduct, but to bad. Do you wish to have no fear of the authority? Then do what is good, and you will receive its approval; for it is God's servant for your good. But if you do what is wrong, you should be

afraid, for the authority does not bear the sword in vain! It is the servant of God to execute wrath on the wrongdoer. Therefore one must be subject, not only because of wrath but also because of conscience. For the same reason you also pay taxes, for the authorities are God's servants, busy with this very thing. Pay to all what is due them – taxes to whom taxes are due, revenue to whom revenue is due, respect to whom respect is due, honor to whom honor is due.

(NRSV)

Romans 13 in the United States

Jeff Sessions and his colleagues might not be aware of it, but in choosing this passage to defend government actions, they actually sided with the loyalists to the British Crown against the Founding Fathers of their nation. Loyalists to King George III cited Paul's words, along with 1 Pet. 2.13–17, to repudiate the revolutionaries for waging war against Britain. None other than John Wesley, founder of Methodism, called on them to repent of their 'sin of rebellion' and to 'fear God and honour the king' (1 Pet. 2.17; Byrd 2013: 118). Another Methodist John Fletcher, in his influential book, *The Bible and the Sword*, warned the colonists: 'St. Paul, who knew the gospel better than English mystics and American patriots, asserts the lawfulness of using the sword in order to maintain good government and execute justice.' Fletcher had in mind Romans 13.4, which in the *King James Version* read '[the king] beareth not the sword in vain: for he is the Minister of God, a Revenger to Execute wrath upon him that doeth evil'. Accordingly Fletcher deemed the king guilty of negligence if he did not wield the sword for sake of quelling rebellion and maintaining social order, for it was indeed his responsibility 'to execute wrath upon criminals' (Byrd 2013: 119).

A few years after the outbreak of conflict, New York minister Charles Inglis, who would later become the first Anglican bishop of Nova Scotia, the new home of the loyalists, preached a sermon entitled *The Duty of Honouring the King*. In it Inglis railed against the 'Horrors of Rebellion' brought on by the 'Sons of Rebellion' who were driven by a 'Phrenzy of Enthusiasm' and 'Republican Ambition'. Lest they be accused of 'making Religion the Cloak of Disloyalty', they must heed the Apostles' words, which enjoined Christians to fear God and to honour the king (Byrd 2013: 120–2;

Noll 2016: 281–2).[1] In answer to the revolutionaries' contention that King Charles was a tyrant, Inglis stated that civic duty must be fulfilled regardless of the king's character, for Paul demanded that Christians obey their ruler, he judged, precisely because the ruler in question was none other than Nero, persecutor of Christians. To the loyalists, 'rulers were God's ministers, God's chosen leaders. No matter what crimes rulers may have committed, God had placed them in power and entrusted them with authority. To disobey them was to revolt against God' no matter what their character might be (Byrd 2013: 122).

Inglis stressed that obedience to the king be absolute, because the insurrectionists had preached that, when Paul spoke of submission to governing authorities, he could not have meant all kings and magistrates, only those who demonstrated just character. That was in fact the argument of Unitarian Jonathan Mayhew, who taught that the ruler was 'the minister of God to thee for good' (Rom. 13.4 KJV), but only if he discharged his duty correctly. In that case disobedience to an unjust ruler would not be 'merely a *political* sin, but a heinous *offense against God* and *religion*'. His crucial qualification to obedience implied that it would not be disobedience to stand up to a tyrant who abused his God-ordained authority (Byrd 2013: 124 emphasis original; Noll 2016: 267–70). The Massachusetts preacher Zabdiel Adams made a similar argument: Paul never advocated 'unreserved obedience' to rulers, only that God-ordained just kings and fair governments (Byrd 2013: 126; Kidd 2014). The regimental chaplain David Griffith made this absolute, stating baldly, '[Paul] never meant… to give sanction to the crimes of wicked and despotic men' (Mullen 2018). Preachers in support of separatists were following the highly influential manifesto by the Connecticut clergyman, judge, legislator Elisha Williams. Understood properly, Williams wrote, Romans 13 taught that '[religious and the civil authorities'] power is a limited one; and therefore the obedience is a limited obedience' (Noll 2016: 264).

Other strategies were deployed to weaken a literal reading of Romans 13. One was to identify the 'governing authorities' of Rom. 13.1 as the higher powers of laws, laws that would be as binding to princes and kings as to commoners (so David Jones in 1775; Byrd 2013: 127). Another, perhaps

---

[1] The charge of making 'Religion the Cloak of Disloyalty' was levelled against Roman Jews, whom Inglis accused of being rebellious and from whom, he insisted, Peter and Paul had commanded the Christians to separate themselves. Inglis's argument was based on both Rom. 13.1–7 and 1 Pet. 2.17.

their best, was to appeal to the overall characters of Peter and Paul, who like Daniel, Shadrach, Meshach, and Abednego of old could not have subjected himself to unjust kings passively and certainly would not have taught others to do so (Byrd 2013: 127–8). The apostle who admonished Christians to 'Stand fast therefore in the liberty wherewith Christ hath made us free' (Gal. 5.1 KJV) could not have suggested that we wilfully submit to enslavement and tyranny (Byrd 2013: 129–36). So the Presbyterian John Zubly stated, 'Freedom is the very spirit and temper of the gospel' (Byrd 2013: 129).

That supporters of the Revolutionary War had to appeal to other biblical passages as well as Paul's overall character to blunt the impact of Romans 13 reveals the weakness of their position. It shows that they were unable to meet the exegetical challenges presented by the passage head on and had to resort to a pattern of broader biblical themes constructed on the basis of context and historical background to make their case. To a general public habituated to treating the Bible as the literal word of God, that could not but appear as a piece of overly subtle sophistry.

The same dynamic was to play out three quarters of a century later when a similar debate was pursued over the legitimacy of slavery. When abolitionists condemned the 1850 Fugitive Slave Act, the so-called 'Bloodhound Law', which required all runaway slaves to be returned to their masters upon capture, for being contrary to the law of God, pro-slavery preachers countered that since slavery was sanctioned and approved by Scripture, it was the Christian duty to submit to the governing authorities that passed the law (Mullen 2018). So, Congregational minister William Mitchell, citing Romans 13, preached that 'civil government, however corrupt, is an institution of God' and therefore must be obeyed (Gehrz 2017). If the decision whether to follow the law were left to personal whims, that would lead to anarchy, which, in the words of another minister, Asa Donaldson of Illinois, would be no better than 'the worst of human governments' (Mullen 2018). Laws passed by the state were by default sacred, and violation of such laws would be considered a violation of God's order: 'These *Christians* in the free States set up their judgments against that of the Almighty, and blindly strike against all law, order, and right', railed one North Carolina newspaper (Mullen 2018 emphasis original).

As in the earlier debate, arguments in support of slavery had the exegetical upper hand, if only because they had a lower hurdle to clear. Proponents of slavery needed only to insist that the text be read literally. To mitigate the general public's tendency of taking Romans 13 at face value, the abolitionists must either go behind the text to consign slavery to an outdated history or, alternatively, place the text within a larger framework of the apostle's attitude towards the institution of slavery. Their hermeneutical principles were based more on reason, a product of the Enlightenment, than on the text. That was the substance of Orson Murray's response to Mitchell: 'I am altogether willing to attribute the monstrous heresy [of slavery] to "blindness of mind" – the habit of taking upon trust long received opinions – rather than to perverseness of heart' (Gehrz 2017).

Appeal to reason had its risks, however, because it was open to the charge of rejecting the 'inerrant' words of the Bible by attacking the very foundation of scripture. That was the gist of the criticism levelled against the abolitionists by the editor of Richmond's *Daily Dispatch*:

> If any and every man in the community chooses to consider any law unscriptural, it is their duty to disobey it – a principle which, if carried into practice, would of course lead at once to rebellion and anarchy. The true doctrine on this subject is set forth in the words of Inspiration itself – 'Let every soul be subject unto the higher powers. For there is no power but of God: the powers that be are ordained of God. Wherefore ye must needs be subject, not only for wrath, but also for conscience sake'[2]
>
> (Gehrz 2017)

Given the religious climate of mid-nineteenth-century America, any appearance of compromising on biblical authority almost certainly guaranteed its rejection. In the last analysis, the American revolutionaries and the abolitionists lost their exegetical skirmishes, even if they were eventually granted their ultimate victories by history.

Romans 13 in Nazi Germany

Paul's words in Rom. 13.1–7 also presented an intractable problematic to the Protestant churches under Nazi Germany. The state made no official pronouncements on the passage, but it did not have to. Its relation to the Protestant church had always been close – so close that few were surprised by the Protestant pastors' support of the Nazis. Supporting ministers made

---

[2] For the nineteenth-century hermeneutical debate between pro-slavery preachers and abolitionists, see Mark Noll (2006).

particular use of Romans 13 to ease the people's misgivings about the country's turn towards authoritarianism. The 1933 Reichstag Fire had set in motion a string of draconian decrees aimed at concentrating more and more power in the hands of the regime. Barely three weeks later, the German theologian Otto Dibelius urged Germans to throw their support behind the new government by citing Martin Luther, who had argued on the basis of Romans 13 that rulers had an obligation to put down rebellions, impose order, and stop the bloodshed by any means (Kraft 2018 citing Thomas Weber). It would be 'sinful' if they failed to do so. Christians by implication would be held accountable if they withheld support for the state, Dibelius said, even if they thought the state was unjust. The sermon was delivered before the newly elected members of a pro-Nazi parliament. Three days later, the Reichstag passed the Enable Act giving Hitler plenary power to pass any law without approval from the parliament. That fall, the German Christians (*Deutsche Christen*) took over the Protestant Confederation to form the German Evangelical Church, and pro-Nazi pastor Ludwig Müller was installed as its first Reich Bishop. One of Müller's first acts was to raise the Swastika at the All Saints' Church in Wittenberg, where Luther had posted his ninety-five theses, thus co-opting the Reformation into Nazi ideology. In a coordinated effort, the Wittenberg Synod passed the Aryan paragraph authorizing the German Evangelical Church to remove all personnel with Jewish ancestry from their posts.

There was resistance among Protestants, to be sure, but it was overshadowed by the 'tens of thousands of sermons up and down the country' by pro-Nazi pastors expounding on Romans 13, which 'became one of the glues that held the Third Reich together' (Weber 2018). Paul's words exerted such influence on the mindset of the Protestant church that, according to historian Thomas Weber, they succeeded in dissuading or at least delaying systematic resistance against the Nazis (Weber 2018). The struggle of Weimar officer Heinrich Graf von Lehndorff, who paid with his life for his participation in the assassination plot of Hitler, illustrates this dilemma perfectly. In his last conversation with his cousin on a lonely train platform a few days before his death, von Lehndorff confessed to being crippled by Paul's foreboding words:

> Must a Christian in his responsibility for his fatherland really have to put up with everything? Must he continue to look on idly as a madman ripped the people into pieces? One thing became clear to us at least: the Apostle Paul gave us no handle if we were to call on his letter to the Romans to save our

own salvation. He only let us know how heavily weighed the decision we are confronted by. There was only a choice between guilt and guilt.

(von Lehndorff 1961: 93 my translation)

Paul's teaching on submitting to the state presented a near-insuperable obstacle to the German Protestant resistance because of the common assumption shared by both sides of the debate: namely, a legitimate challenge to the state must be based not on reason, as in the case of American abolitionists, but on the institutional church. Otto Dibelius alluded to this point in his 1933 sermon: 'From Rev. Martin Luther we learned that the church should not be allowed to interfere with legitimate state power if it does what it is called to do, even if it turns hard and ruthless' (Weber 2018). Karl Barth, in an extended discussion of Romans 13, likewise stressed the centrality of the church in resistance against an abusive state. Barth argued that the injunction 'be subject to the governing authorities' was directed to the church but only in its capacity of fulfilling the priestly mission of 'free preaching of justification'; the injunction must not be taken to mean submitting absolutely or abstractly to all governments in all situations (Barth 1939: 64–6).

Church and State, Barth maintained, must be sharply distinguished one from the other, because they fulfil different functions in a divinely ordained order: 'In this very close relation between the existence of the Church and that of the State, the Church cannot itself become a State, and the State… cannot become a Church' (Barth 1939: 45). When a state tries to 'strengthen its authority by making any kind of *inward* claim upon its subjects and its citizens' or 'to demand from them a particular philosophy of life (*Weltanschauung*), or at least sentiments and reactions dominated by a particular view imposed by the State from without', then the state arrogates to itself the role of a church and usurps its identity. That is because, he said, '*love* is *not* one of the duties which we owe to the State… When the State begins to claim "love" it is in process of becoming a Church, the Church of a false God, and thus an unjust State. The just State requires, not love, but a simple, resolute and responsible attitude on the part of its citizens' (Barth 1939: 76–7 emphasis original). In the event that the state abuses its God-given authority by demanding what only the church can demand, the church must not shirk its responsibility of resisting the state – openly and publicly. There are boundaries to the state's authority as laid out in the hierarchical structure of Rom. 13.1, in other words, and it is the responsibility of the church to call the state back to the properly ordained order. In that case, there is no better way to honour the state than to level justified criticism against it:

> Christians would, in point of fact, become enemies of any State if, when the State threatens their freedom, they did not resist, or if they concealed their resistance – although this resistance would be very calm and dignified. Jesus would, in actual fact, have been an enemy of the State if He had not dared, quite calmly, to call King Herod a 'fox' (Luke xiii. 32). If the State has perverted its God-given authority, it cannot be honored better than by this *criticism* which is due to it in all circumstances.

> (Barth 1939: 69 emphasis original)

The English title, which accurately reflects the content of the book, translates the original German title, *Rechtfertigung und Recht*, which literally means 'Justification and Justice'. This easy transition from the theological to the social and political is indicative of Barth's church-centred conception of the state.

Barth's interpretation of Romans 13 was influential among those who were desperately looking for exegetical resources to resist the menace of sweeping authoritarianism. It moved the plotters of the assassination attempt on Hitler in 1944 (Weber 2018) and inspired Dietrich Bonhoeffer to turn against Hitler, a decision that would end in his execution two weeks before the arrival of American troops. Bonhoeffer's own reading of Romans 13 was similarly grounded in the church as the locus of all interactions with the state:

> The starting-point of St. Paul's thinking is always the church, and his sole concern is its well-being and manner of life. So much so, he feels obliged to warn the Christians to refrain from any unjust or evil conduct themselves, but does not utter a single word of reproach to the State… On no account must evil occur within the Church. Once again, St. Paul is talking to the Christians, not the State. His concern is that the Christians should persevere in repentance and obedience wherever they may be and whatever conflict should threaten them.

> (Bonhoeffer 1959: 294)

Paul demanded obedience from the church, contended Bonhoeffer, not because the worldly governments were good 'but because the Church must obey the will of God, whether the State be good or bad' (Bonhoeffer 1959: 294).

Bonhoeffer's injunction to do good irrespective of the character of the state ended up backing the church into an ethical corner, however, for it left the church little room for resistance against an abusive regime. A construction of submission within the framework of the church's priestly function might shield it from blind obedience to the state, but if obedience to an earthly government was not absolute, then neither could resistance against an evil regime. At the end, the best Bonhoeffer could muster was an argument from silence: Because Romans 13 has in mind the church exclusively, 'no state is entitled to read into St. Paul's words a justification of its own existence' (Bonhoeffer 1959: 294). The powerlessness of the church was borne out by historical events of the 1930s. Conscientious pastors, in opposition to the state church, had formed the Confessing Church in 1933, of which Bonhoeffer was an early member and for which Barth composed the Barman Declaration of 1934. But the Confessing Church remained so ineffective that Bonhoeffer finally decided to renounce his membership as he contemplated joining the assassination plot.

Barth's position on the church's role in resisting the state fared better, though ultimately it too proved powerless to overcome the explicit command of submission. Both Church and State were part of an 'order' (*taxis*),[3] according to Barth, within which they found their assigned but distinct roles, but it was an order created and maintained by God, not by the church or the state (Barth 1939: 65). Thus, the church must acknowledge the power of the state given by God even if that meant suffering injustice; opposing the state would be tantamount to opposing the power of God. Barth left room for resistance against an abusive state, but that could be exercised only in context of respect for the God-ordained power granted to the state:

> But this respect for the authority of the State… cannot possibly consist of an attitude of abstract and absolute elasticity towards the intentions and undertakings of the State, simply because… the possibility may arise that the power of the State, on its side, may become guilty of opposition to the Lord of lords, to that divine ordinance to which it owes its power. If Christians are still to respect the State, even then, their docility in this instance can only be *passive*, and, as such, *limited*. The 'subjection' can in no case mean that the Church and its members will approve, and wish of their own free will to further, the claims and undertakings of the State, if once the State power is turned not to the protection but to the suppression of the preaching of justification. *Even then Christians will never fail to grant that which is*

---

[3] It should be noted that *taxis* does not actually appear in Romans 13, only its cognates built on the *tass*-stem: *hypotassein* 'to submit' (13.1, 5), *tassein* 'to order, appoint, ordain' (13.1), *antitassein* 'to oppose' (13.2), and *diatagē* 'arrangement, decree, ordinance' (13.2).

indispensable to the State power as guardian of the public law, as an ordained power … even if the State abuses this *exousia* [authority], and demonstrates its opposition, as a demonic power, to the Lord of lords.

(Barth 1939: 66–7 emphasis original)

The reason Barth was willing to grant near-absolute power to the state had to do with his Christological interpretation. Depending on earlier scholars, Barth understood 'authorities' of Rom. 13.1 to be the same angelic beings as mentioned in 1 Cor. 15.24; Col. 1.16; 2.10, 15; Eph. 1.21; 3.10; 6.12; 1 Pet. 3.22, etc., which were created in and for Christ and will, in the end time, be gathered into Christ (1 Cor. 15.24; Barth 1939: 23–9).[4] This meant, for Barth, 'that power, the State as such, belongs originally and ultimately to Jesus Christ; that in its comparatively independent substance, in its dignity, its function and its purpose, it should serve the Person and the Work of Jesus Christ and therefore the justification of the sinner' (Barth 1939: 29). This near-deification of the state made it practically impossible for the church to stage any meaningful resistance against the Nazi regime. It was also a misappropriation of the angelology of nations, as later scholars conclusively showed (Strobel 1956; Käsemann 1969a: 204).

This Christological interpretation of the state is of a piece with his apocalyptical view first expounded in his famous commentary on the Romans. In the end time, according to Barth, when the existing order is dissolved into the Father, the 'Primal Order of God', which functions as a mathematical 'minus sign', will negate the totality of all existence and all present orders, including church, law, society, state, and government:

All human consciousness, all human principles and axioms and orthodoxies and -isms, all *principality and power and dominion*, are AS SUCH subjected to the destructive judgement of God. *Let every man be in subjection* means, therefore, that every man should consider the falsity of all human reckoning as such.

(Barth 1933: 111–12 emphasis original)

Such a view was capable of mounting powerful critiques against absolute claims and messianic pretensions made by the state. But as a basis for organizing and coordinating resistance against an authoritarian regime that

---

[4] Barth took issue with translating *katargein* of 1 Cor. 15.24 as 'annihilate', because in the next verse Christ assumes sovereignty over 'every ruler, every authority and power', not destroys them (Barth 1939: 26).

would not hesitate for a moment using extreme violence to destroy the very forum that makes critiques possible, Barth's view of the state failed miserably, as history demonstrated. It encouraged a form of apocalyptic passivity even as it granted the state divinely ordained authority.

Wrestling with Romans 13 Today

On the 'theological problem' that was the American Civil War, Mark Noll attributes the defeat of the antislavery hermeneutics to a reading public demanding simple literalist adherence to the inerrant Bible:

> [The antislavery] position could not simply be read out of any one biblical text; it could not be lifted directly from the page. Rather, it needed patient reflection on the entirety of the Scriptures; it required expert knowledge of the historical circumstances of ancient Near Eastern and Roman slave systems as well as of the actually existing conditions in the slave states; and it demanded that sophisticated interpretive practice replace a commonsensically literal approach to the sacred text. In short, *this was an argument of elites requiring that the populace defer to its intellectual betters.*
>
> (Noll 2006: 49 emphasis added)

The use of Rom. 13.1–7, at least in the West, to support slavery is unsurprising, for the Bible in general has frequently been interpreted to support the state. Chrysostom thought Romans 13 demanded that Christians compromise with rulers no matter how tyrannical, authoritarian, or unjust they might be (*Homilies on Romans* 23; Landes 1982: 41–3). Those unconvinced by his reading sought to restrain the passage's seeming absoluteness by pairing it with Acts 5.29, 'We must obey God rather than humans' (Burns 2012). In face of an intolerable government, Augustine advocated separation or quietism, retreat from engaging the state (*On Romans* 72; Landes 1982: 41–3; Dunn 1986). Western Christians have never been able to derive support for resistance against unjust rulers from this passage.

Today, however, in the wake of a century of genocides and massive exterminations launched by murderous regimes, history has reached a decisive judgement: No matter how the passage might have been appropriated in the past, it can no longer be used to provide biblical basis for blind obedience to the state. The distrust of those in power is so great, and absolute submission to authority so bankrupt, that the only reading strategy that seems viable is one that must involve 'patient reflection' on the biblical text, 'expert knowledge' of the first-century social and political world, and 'sophisticated interpretive practice', the very qualities nineteenth-century Americans rejected. To read Rom. 13.1–7 responsibly – or 'ethically' in the way that Elisabeth Schüssler Fiorenza has suggested (Schüssler Fiorenza 1988) – is to do so *contextually*, which is to say, to interpret the passage in the context of the overall arguments in Romans, Paul's thoughts in general, and the social and political world of the first century.

One reason why Paul's command to submit to governing authorities are so difficult to swallow is that they seem at odds with his criticisms against earthly authorities and institutions elsewhere in his writings. With his expectation of the imminent return of Christ, the world with all its kingdoms and states will be delivered to the Father by demolishing 'every rule and *authority* and power' (1 Cor. 15.24). The use of the term 'authority' in 1 Corinthians is especially relevant, since it is the same term used in Romans 13. Accordingly, the believers' citizenship is in heaven and they should not be attached to earthly things (Phil. 3.20). His injunction to submit to governing authorities and to grant them honour is ever starker when seen in the immediate context of Romans 12–15 (Elliott 1997b: 186). In this so-called ethical section, Paul presents the world as a fallen order after the first Adam (following the conclusion of Romans 8) by issuing the explicit warning 'not to conform to this age' (Rom. 12.2). This 'monumental contradiction' (Furnish 1979: 117) proves so vexing that some have resorted to dismissing the whole passage as a non-Pauline interpolation (Kallas 1965).

We are on surer ground when we set Paul's words in the context of 'the imperial situation' imposed by Roman colonialism (Horsley 1987: 1–19), which exerted influence on all the writers of the New Testament (Georgi 1991: 81–104; Elliott 1994: 214–16, 2000: 17–39). Under the terms of *Pax Romana* the overlords dictated a narrative that presented themselves as benevolent conquerors and a policy that offered peace, with the constant threat of violence, in exchange for submission. That narrative affected the subjects, however, not only in what was intended – maintaining imperial superiority – but also in what was unintended – instilling in the subjects a language of power and domination that they mimicked and adapted for their own purpose of resisting the mighty Empire. The imperial narrative was, therefore, a form of doublespeak that the ruled could deploy against the rulers themselves who invented it and propagated it throughout the Empire.

Evidence for this doublespeak is the presence of terms and concepts in Rom. 13.1–7 that are capable of conveying meanings at two distinct levels depending on whether they were heard by the ruling class or by the ruled. As demonstrated in the introduction, the Roman congregation was composed of almost exclusively resident aliens (*peregrini*). That means ruling elites were outsiders unversed in biblical worldview or symbols of Jewish monotheism. Rulers and elites would be eager to see their values confirmed and their elevated status acknowledged to begin with; without the keys to unlock the Paul's complex references, they would have certainly heard the command to submit to governing authorities as a consolidation of the worldview they constructed for themselves: namely, a world in which they by nature are entitled to their superior positions in relation to their adoring subjects. To insiders, however, who were habituated by their alien status, heavy tax burden, and overall disenfranchisement but shared Paul's language and worldview or at least were in a position to decode them, they would have understood that absolute submission could be rendered properly only to God, the Authority of the universe who was the fountainhead of all other earthly authorities and before whom all governing authorities must submit themselves.

For these two levels of meaning to coexist in the same text and to be conveyed by the same words, they must be kept consciously distinct from each other, if nothing else, simply to protect those below. Those in power must never find out that words they took to be supportive of their hold to power could in fact be disguised ridicules of their status and criticisms of their dominance. To achieve this, these words were coded to disguise their true intent. Paul's rhetoric might appear to ruling elites as advocating submission and docile subservience, an interpretation that would reinforce their views of themselves as the natural, entitled leaders and reassure them that no revolution or social upheaval was being fomented. Insiders, on the other hand, who shared Paul's language and belief and who were conscious of their own status as permanent subordinates, would come to the opposite conclusion. Paul's words would appear to them as a subversive text in disclosing an underlying structure of reality in which their God was the final arbiter of power and alone had the authority to grant legitimacy of all temporal authorities.

This coded message not only made it possible for the resident aliens to make sense of their lowly status in society but also empowered them to eagerly expect the final triumph of God in Jesus, as recounted in Romans 8.

This shared secrecy in midst of public contempt they all experienced in their daily life thus informed their communal identity and shaped them into a close-knit group. That fits in well with the overarching theme of Romans 12–15, whose concerns have to do with practical life of the congregation (Dunn 1988b: 759).

How hearers understood the text therefore depended on their station in society, and self-selected hermeneutics succeeded in isolating these two classes of hearers from each other, thus protecting the weak from the strong, the powerless from the powerful. The self-identified powerful would understand Rom. 13.1–7 from the top down in a move mirroring how they viewed themselves in the imperial hierarchy. The powerless, with their full knowledge of the coded message in these words, would understand Paul's words from the bottom up.[5]

Reading Paul from the Top Down

The ruling elites would have been captivated by the opening call for submission to the 'governing authorities' (Rom. 13.1). 'Authority' (*exousia*) had a wide range of meanings, from 'freedom' to 'capability to perform an action', and implied the presence of power to accomplish what others could not. From this the word, in the plural, acquired a secondary sense of 'authoritative position', 'office of a state', 'office-bearers', or 'rulers' (Foerster 1964: 562–3; Delling 1972a: 29; Liddell-Scott-Jones 1968: 599; BDAG 2000: 352–4). The historian Josephus, for example, used 'authorities' to refer to local magistrates and officials (Josephus, *War* 2.350; Jewett 2006: 787–8).

Incidentally, if *exousia* included an implied government or state only in a derivative sense, it seems a stretch to claim that Paul was espousing 'a major political statement about government' (Blumenfeld 2001: 391 n272). Instead, in dealing with such concrete forms of political power as rates and taxes, more likely Paul had in mind local magistrates and government officials rather than any grand theory about power of the state: 'Any glorification of political power is conspicuous by its absence' (Käsemann 1969a: 202–3). It might therefore be more accurate to see Paul's 'political realism' at work in this passage (Dunn 1986: 67). Furthermore, Paul here was concerned with how recipients of his letter should act and behave towards the government

---

[5] Previous efforts of reading Rom. 13.1–7 at two levels can be found in Wan (2008) and Harrison (2011: 313). Gaventa (2017) has also taken a subtle approach along a similar line.

and what responsibilities they bore as resident aliens in the seat of the Empire; he otherwise said nothing to the ruling elites and government officials. It would be a monstrous distortion for those in power to use Paul's words to demand blind obedience to the state.

The expression *exousiai hyperechousai* is found nowhere else in ancient literature, and its combination of two words both meaning more or less the same thing is odd. The participle *hyperechousai/hyperechontes*, literally 'superior, surpassing', was frequently used as a synonym for 'those in power' (BDAG 2000: 1033), with an implied meaning of social and political prominence (Isocrates, *Oratio* 4.95; Aristotle, *Politics* 3.1284a37; Delling 1972b: 523). In the only other political usage of the term in the New Testament, the author of 1 Peter demands that a king be acknowledged as 'superior' (2.13). The ruling elites would have understood the expression as a redundant reference to government officials. This excess of meaning could well have been taken in 'a cumulative sense that encompasses a range of officials placed in superior positions of political authority, duly appointed to their tasks and currently exercising their power' (Jewett 2006: 788).

With the opening line thus co-opted, the ruling elites could then proceed to interpret the rest of the passage within their privileged framework. They would have read 'rulers' (13.3), which Paul elsewhere used in the sense of 'angelic powers' in 1 Corinthians 2, as 'public officials' corresponding to *consul* or *praefectus* in the Roman administrative system (Dunn 1988b: 763; Blumenfeld 2001). 'Good work' and 'evil work' of 13.4 would then be taken not in the moral sense but as referring to conducts in a political arena (Käsemann 1980: 353). 'Minister' (*diakonos*), used twice in 13.4, was a well-known office in the emergent Jesus-movement and was mentioned numerous times by Paul, but it would have been taken by the ruling class simply to be government officials. *Leitourgos* (13.6), literally 'liturgist or servant', was another cultic word Paul used elsewhere (e.g. Phil. 2.25), even in Romans (15.16), but its cultic reference would have been overshadowed by its usage in the context of government. There is ample evidence outside early Christian literature that both *diakonos* and *leitourgos* meant first of all civic officials or functionaries. *Leitourgos* was a civil servant in charge of collecting taxes in Classical Athens, which is the exact context of Rom. 13.6. It was used later to refer to officials who provided services to a political body (Strobel 1956: 86–7; Strathmann and Meyer 1967: 216–18). The king's ministers were called *diakonoi* in the Septuagint (Esther 1.10; 2.2; 6.3; Strathmann and Meyer 1967: 231; Dunn 1988b: 764). Both *diakonos* and *leitourgos* were in fact used interchangeably in the Septuagint for political officers (e.g. 2 Sam. 13.18; 1 Kings 10.5; Sir. 10.2).

Given the widespread usage of these terms in civil government, the elites could perhaps be excused for taking Paul's words at face value as confirmation of their self-understanding as benevolent public servants. Service was disdained in the ancient world, especially by the Sophists (Plato, *Gorgias* 491e), but it would acquire a higher value if it was rendered to the state, and then only voluntarily and without remuneration (Plato, *Laws* 955c-d). 'The statesman rules as *a minister* of the city, not for the sake of ruling nor for the sake of its own desires, but for the sake of the service laid upon him, which consists supremely in the education of good citizens' (Beyer 1964: 82). What is more, the elites found themselves designated servants *of God*, a title that was reinforced by their self-understanding. According to Roman political theology, the Empire had been established and enlarged by heavenly heroes (Cicero, *Rep.* 6.13), and the Romans had been given a divine mandate to rule the peoples of the earth and to pacify them by conquest (*Aeneid* 6.851–53). In Hellenistic political philosophy, the ruler was touted an 'imitator and servant of God' (Sthenidas, *On Kingship;* Blumenfeld 2001: 254–5).

The elites would likewise interpret Paul's copious language of submission as promoting dutiful acquiescence, good citizenship, and most importantly acceptance of their eminence. The verbs 'to be subject' (*hypotassesthai,* 13.1, 5) and 'to resist' (*antitassesthai,* 13.2) and the noun 'order, command, ordinance' (*diatagē,* 13.2) are cognates of *tassesthai* ('to be ordered, instituted'; 13.1). That these closely related words are compacted in the opening verses of this passage would point to the construction of a unified order: namely, 'those authorities that exist have been *instituted by God*' (13.1). *Tassesthai* is a military term denoting the arrangement of the rank and file for battle (Delling 1972a: 27; Liddell-Scott-Jones 1996: 1759), but it could also be used in the context of officials' being appointed for certain political positions (e.g. LXX 2 Sam. 7.11; Tob. 1.21; Jewett 2006: 789). The use of *diatagē* and *antitassesthai* would have been understood as reinforcing that order, and *hypotassesthai* as acknowledging the supremacy of the governing authorities.

That God could use foreign leaders to fulfil divine purpose is a common theme in the Bible. Persian King Cyrus, who did not even know the LORD by name, was appointed a messiah, 'God's anointed', to subdue the Babylonians and to conquer all peoples, in order to free the Jewish exiles and grant them return to their native land (Isa. 45.1–13). Nevertheless, anyone familiar with biblical reasoning would also be aware that just as God could appoint hostile adversaries to fulfil God's purpose, they could just as easily be deposed once the purpose is fulfilled. As with the case of Nebuchadnezzar, his kingdom existed at God's pleasure, and its very existence served as an affirmation of God's authority over the king (Daniel 4). Such a view of foreign powers is especially prevalent in the Wisdom tradition (e.g. Sir. 10.4; Wis. 6.1–11). For unsuspecting Roman officials unschooled in biblical reasoning, however, this subtlety would have been lost on them. For them it was enough that the passage appears to support the right of the government to bear arms, to exercise police action (13.4), and to collect taxes (13.6–7). They would have concluded that Paul had reached a resolution, grudgingly perhaps, to support members of the ruling class by integrating them into his religious system. They would have been convinced that it was Paul's intention to maintain peace.

Reading from the Bottom Up

How might insiders, the intended recipients, the disadvantaged resident aliens, have understood Paul's admonition? They would have heard the same terms against a background formed by Paul's other writings and reached vastly different conclusions. They would have noted, first of all, that Paul's use of many cognates of the *tass*-root could not have been an accident. They would have understood he deliberately chose to avoid using *hypakouein*, 'to obey', to make his case. *Hypakouein* (Rom. 6.12, 16; 10.16) and the related noun *hypakoē* (Rom. 1.5; 5.19; 6.16; 15.18; 16.19, 26) would have suggested absolute obedience, as when Paul demands that one not dedicate one's body in obedience to sin's passion (Rom. 6.12, 16). Paul's deliberate use of *hypotassesthai* suggests instead that an order (*taxis* or *tagma*) underlies the current political relationship and that this order is undergirded by divine fiat. 'Paul looks out on a world in which superiors and subordinates exist and intends his readers to come to terms with this reality', as Ernst Käsemann (1969a: 2070) observed, but that is a divine reality whose creator and sustainer is none other than the God of Israel. In that linguistic universe, insiders would have heard *hypotassesthai* in the sense of 'ordering oneself' into an existing pattern, a pattern that is instituted by God, rather than in the sense of submitting to some civil authorities (Lehmann 1975: 302 n. 45; Boesak 1986: 146).

Paul used the verb *hypotassein* thirteen times outside of Rom. 13.1, 5. In the five times the verb is used in the active voice, God is the subject (Rom.

8.20; 1 Cor. 15.27 [2x], 28; Phil. 3.21). Eight times the verb is used in the middle or passive voice (Rom. 8.7, 20; 10.3; 1 Cor. 14.32; 15.27, 28 [2x]; 16.16); all but three of them refer to submitting to God. The fleshly mind is not subject to God's law (Rom. 8.7), unbelieving Israel does not subject itself to God's righteousness (Rom. 10.3), and in the end time, all things will be placed in subjection to the Son, after which the Son would submit himself to the Father (1 Cor. 15.27–28). In two other places submission to God is at least implied. In Rom. 8.20 God is said to subject creation to futility involuntarily, and in 1 Cor. 14.32 early prophets are asked to take responsibility for the manner in which they prophesy in worship, for the spirits of the prophets ultimately are subject to them (Dunn 1988a: 427). Some have stressed the voluntary nature of Paul's use of *hypotassein* as if one could withhold submission to tyrants and abusive rulers at any time (Porter 1990: 121–2), but this survey makes clear that Paul does allow for involuntary submission as well. The decaying creation (Rom. 8.20) or the fleshly thought cannot submit itself to the law of God (Rom. 8.7), because Paul's thought is grounded in the sovereignty of the Jewish monotheistic God who is independent of human will.

The only exceptions to God not being the recipient of submission are found only in 1 Cor. 16.15–16, where Paul exhorts his audience to subject themselves to Stephanas and his household who commanded their respect because 'they have *devoted* themselves' (*etaxan heautous*) to the service of the holy ones. This meaning of *tassein* with a reflexive pronoun as 'to devote [oneself to certain task]' is well attested in ancient literature (Xenophon, *Memorabilia Socratis* 2.1.11; Plato, *Republic* 2.371c), and its combination with *hypotassethai* forms a close parallel to Rom. 13.1. In both passages Paul uses direct speech to enjoin submission to human leaders as opposed to God before adducing reasons why such submission would be proper and legitimate. To 'the governing authorities' Paul advocates submission, because their authority is derived ultimately from God. In the case of Stephanas and his household, submission is warranted because of their labour for the holy ones. In both cases, human leaders have no intrinsic authority of their own; they command submission only because they are performing work for God's elect.

From an examination of Paul's submission language a pattern emerges. Absolute submission is rendered legitimately only to God; submission to human actors is legitimate only when they are rightfully appointed by God. This principle is in fact stated explicitly in the opening verse of Romans 13: 'Let every person be subject to the governing authorities; for *there is no authority except from God*, and those authorities that exist *have been instituted by God*' (Rom. 13.1). Those who submitted themselves to temporal authorities do so from a reasoned position. They act not out of fear or blind faith in human institutions but on the basis of a clear-eyed evaluation of the origins of that authority. That is why Paul contrasts fear to conscience as motivation for submission (13.5). Submission to the governing authorities is warranted if and only if God is acknowledged to be the true source of authority. Government officials command our respect only insofar as they are appointed by God and serve as God's representatives.

A passage that publicly urged submission to local magistrates therefore encodes a hidden message that only insiders can decode with a wink and a nod. Government officials to whom respect is due are therefore placed under the absolute authority of God – that is to say, the God of Jesus and the patriarchs, not of Zeus or Apollo. Bruno Blumenfeld aptly captures the mood of this co-optation:

> Paul's deftness in manipulating the system by working against its self-negating proclivities is so successful as to camouflage his own wit when castigating its representatives. Throughout Rom. 13.1–7, the irony is veiled (to incomprehension) as a political stereotype. "Fear the governing officials" may sound as an irreproachable advice to the authorities' ear but, these are, unbeknown to themselves, slaves to God as well.
>
> (Blumenfeld 2001: 391–2 n. 273)

What Blumenfeld means by 'incomprehension' is in fact intentional opacity and dissemblance designed to trick those who were in power. For members of the Roman congregation, *peregrini* who have been denied citizen rights but nevertheless are saddled with the Empire's tax burdens, their recourse is resistance that is encoded in biblical language. Paul does his part by misleading unsuspecting government officials by using common administrative terms that have radically different meanings in the context of biblical worldview to produce two messages to be heard at different levels. One is intended for public consumption, to be pursued within the calculating logic of the dominant class. The other is the intended discourse between Paul his audience, the underclass of Roman society.

Coded Resistance

James C. Scott calls these two levels the public and hidden scripts of political discourse (Scott 1985, 1990: 2–18; Herzog 1994: 341–2). Discourses between any partners of unequal power, as between the ruling class and their subordinates, are often constructed on two levels. There is the public script based on the separation between these two classes that choreographs the interaction between masters and subjects, but such a script is put together by the elites to reinforce the values of the master class and to legitimate their rule. In that respect, the public script is really a 'self-portrait of dominant elites as they would have themselves seen' (Scott 1990: 18). As a matter of survival, the underclass must feign obedience by playing along, obsequiously and ostensibly following the public script on stage, all the while writing their own script of the same events off stage. The script from below must be hidden from the ruling class, but this 'hidden script contains what the oppressed say to each other and think about their rulers' (Herzog 1994: 341). The gulf that exists between the public and the hidden scripts is bridged by a third form of political discourse, what Scott calls 'a politics of disguise and anonymity that takes place in public view but is designed to have a double meaning or to shield the identity of the actors'. In that discourse of resistance, 'a partly sanitized, ambiguous and coded version of the hidden transcript is always present in the public discourse of subordinate groups' (Scott 1990: 18–19). This is the nature of Paul's words in Romans 13.

One device Paul used to disguise his hidden transcript in his public discourse is to shift his language from 'authorities' in the plural to singular 'authority'. Calling attention to the 'governing authorities' with the intentionally redundant phrase *exousiai hyperechousai* (plural) from the start (13.1a), Paul's script slips in a singular usage of *exousia* – not just to describe the true source of authority but especially to exclude the possibility for the existence of authority outside the God of Israel, 'for there is no authority except from God' (13.1b). The governing officials have their positions of power – they are the way they are – only because 'they that exist have been instituted by God' (13.1c). Thus Paul provides a material connection between the officials and God: the officials are portrayed as foot soldiers – using the military word *tassesthai* (literally 'to be placed in formation') – under God's command. Governing elites serve only at the pleasure of God.

The payoff for Paul's distinction between 'authorities' and 'authority' becomes apparent to insiders in the following line: 'Therefore whoever resists *authority* [singular] resists God's order' (Rom. 13.2a). Most commentators, assuming 'authority' here to be synonymous with 'governing authorities' of the previous verse, render 'God's order (*diatagē*)' as 'what God has appointed' (so NRSV) or 'instituted' (NIV), harking back to the phrase 'instituted by God' of the last sentence. That is how the ruling elites would read the verse. They take 13.2 to be a parallel to the opening line, restated negatively here to warn about opposition to the ruling class. This is also the verse that many pro-government exegetes seize on to dismiss opposition against the state, be it in Revolution America, Nazi Germany, or the Trump administration. That misdirection is likely part of Paul's rhetorical strategy – to better disguise his hidden discourse with the Roman congregation. But if the insiders are to carry through this distinction between the plural 'authorities' and singular 'authority' established at the outset, they would read the opposition to authority not as against the state but as against God or, in Paul's language, against 'God's order'. They would understand that this warning is issued to *all* – including government officials who owe their position to the order or formation established by God. Instead of commanding absolute submission to temporal authorities, therefore, Paul in fact subjects all, rulers and the ruled, who without exception receive their marching orders from God, to the one who alone has the authority and power to issue such demands.

The same doublespeak can be observed in 13.3–4 in spite of its more complex pattern of repetition, if we pay close attention to Paul's shift from the plural 'rulers' to the singular 'authority'. These two verses form what one scholar calls 'a practical reason' adduced in support of submission, the practical reason being the natural calculus of avoiding punishment and gaining honour (Stein 1989: 332–6). But as before this injunction is not one-sided but applies to both subjects and rulers. Paul begins with a public praise of benevolent rulers who should not be a terror to good conduct, only to evil (Rom. 13.3a). That is immediately followed by a question, 'Do you wish not to fear the authority?' (13.3b). The shift from the plural 'rulers' to the singular 'authority' helps Paul disguise his hidden script. His imperial censors would approve the question, especially after the positive statement of 13.3a, because it again connects the singular *exousia* to 'governing authorities' with whom they would naturally identify, as do the vast majority of modern readers. Such a reading would, of course, miss the monotheistic foundation for 'authority', which no insiders would. They would instead acknowledge the supreme and singular authority of the God of Jesus and the patriarchs, before whom *all*, even rulers and officials, must fear. A rhetorical question posed to fellow subalterns, publicly before the watchful eyes of the colonizers, thus becomes a charge against the lordly, the mighty, the powerful.

The same misdirection is carried into the next verse: 'for it is a *diakonos* of God for your good. But if you do what is wrong, you should be afraid, for the authority does not bear the sword in vain! It is the responsibility of the *diakonos* [NRSV servant] of God to execute wrath on the wrongdoer' (13.4).

Paul uses no explicit subject for the singular verb 'is' in the first sentence on purpose, because it leaves the identity of the *diakonos* ambiguous and thus helps him disguise his message to the probing eyes of censors. Some translations supply 'the one in authority' (e.g. the NIV), thus identifying the governing authorities as deacons of God. No doubt that is how the ruling elites would hear the sentence as well. Syntactically, however, the most natural candidate for the subject is 'authority' of the last verse, whom Paul, with a nod to his audience, now calls, in a circumlocution, 'deacon of God'. It is this deacon of God who bears a sword of righteousness and justice and who executes judgement, with fairness and alacrity, on all wrongdoers irrespective of their stations in life or status in society. Virtually all modern commentators, with the ruling elites of yore, take 'bearing sword' to refer to the use of police action by the powerful to maintain control over their subjects (Fitzmyer 1993: 668; Jewett 2006: 795), but only the insiders are able to identify accurately the true locus of this absolute authority. They know God alone metes out punishment to all, even the governing authorities themselves.

The care with which Paul folds the hidden script into a public discourse is also evident in the way he uses the title *diakonos*. At first glance, he seems to be calling government officials 'deacon (*diakonos*) of God' twice in 13.4. As noted above, there is precedence for applying the title *diakonos* to a civil official, but his audience know better. Ten times *diakonos* appears in the undisputed letters of Paul outside out Rom. 13.4, and each time it refers to the office of deacon or minister within the burgeoning Jesus-movement. Paul calls himself or his fellow missionaries *diakonoi* on behalf of the good news or the congregation of God: Phoebe (Rom. 16.1), Apollos and himself (1 Cor. 3.5), himself (2 Cor. 3.6), unnamed fellow workers (2 Cor. 6.4; Phil. 1.1). He twice called Christ a *diakonos*, of the 'circumcised' (Rom. 15.8) and, ironically, of sinners (Gal. 2.17; Beyer 1964: 82). When he polemicizes against the 'superior apostles', he does not refrain from calling them *diakonoi* (2 Cor. 11.15 [2x], 23), even though he doubts their authenticity.

Paul often uses the title *diakonos* in conjunction with a possessive. For example, Paul calls Phoebe a *diakonos* 'of a congregation in Cenchreae' (Rom. 16.1), which could mean she either works for that congregation or is commissioned by it. Either way, Paul thinks she deserves respect for her association with that congregation. Paul calls himself a *diakonos* 'for the gospel' (1 Cor. 3.5) and 'of the new covenant' (2 Cor. 3.6). In both instances, the possessive of things (congregation, gospel) defines the task of the deacon. When Paul modified *diakonos* with an agent, he uses it to indicate the master to whom the deacon belonged. It was this category of usage that caused a great deal of controversy between Paul and his detractors. For example, Paul hotly contests the superior apostles' self-designation as '*diakonoi* of Christ', calling them derisively '*diakonoi* of Satan' who disguised themselves as *diakonoi* of righteousness (2 Cor. 11.15). He reserves the title '*diakonos* of Christ' for himself (2 Cor. 11.23), because he contends that his sufferings have earned him that right. When he calls himself a '*diakonos* of God' (2 Cor. 6.4), he recounts his sufferings on behalf of the gospel as proof of his diaconate. In this usage, '*diakonos* of Christ' comes close to his preferred terms 'slave of Christ Jesus' (Rom. 1.1) and the much-contested title 'apostle' (Beyer 1964: 89). Evidently, *diakonos* has become a recognized title in the early Jesus-movement, and it was such a contested title that Paul would not casually apply it to just anyone. Given the special theological weight with which Paul freights *diakonos*, his intended audience would immediately recognize that Paul is not applying the title to officials but uses it as a circumlocution for God (for fuller discussion, see Wan 2008).

Conclusion

In spite of innumerable attempts to soften the compromising tone of the passage, the regnant approach remains that of Paul ceding to earthly rulers full authority, however temporary it might be before the end time (Roetzel 2000: 228; Wan 2000a: 191–215). At most critics grant that for Paul, '[The civil government] is a part of the natural moral order, of divine appointment, but lying outside the order of grace revealed in Christ' (Dodd 1959: 211). This approach to Paul's troubling words in Romans 13 might at first glance seem like political realism; it actually creates an unbearable tension with Paul's attitude towards earthly governments elsewhere. It also has the effect of pressing Paul's words into a single meaning, not allowing him to disguise the true intents of his discourse in face of watchful hostile authorities.

The reading of Romans 13 attempted here proposes a solution by taking serious Paul's own social and political locations in Roman society and those of his audiences. Full weight has been accorded to the power differential between two audiences. To the power elite, those indirectly addressed by Paul, the passage sounds like a concession to the supreme authority of the state, to which believers are counselled obedience and submission, grudgingly perhaps but real regardless. To them, Paul seems willing to go so far as to legitimate the state's functions – chief among them taxation and police control – by appealing to divine ordinance. However well they might understand Paul's Jewish thought, it would be impressive enough that Paul seems to carve out a niche in his theological edifice for foreign government.

Such a theological argument cuts both ways, however. Jesus-followers in Rome, insiders all to Paul's rhetoric and theology, the audience directly addressed in the epistle, are more inclined to understand Paul's argument in traditional biblical and Hellenistic-Jewish terms. The God who tolerates, even ordains, political structures of the world can just as easily overthrow them if they fail to live up to God's expectations. Paul's apocalypticism would radicalize divine judgement even further. Elsewhere he speaks of the powers and authorities of this world drawing to a close in light of the eschatological triumph of Christ (1 Cor. 2.6–8; 15.24). Once grafted into Paul's apocalyptic worldview, political structures are doomed to oblivion. Such a critical stance would be lost on outsiders unschooled in Jewish Wisdom or apocalyptic thoughts. To them, Paul dissembles and disguises his discourse as an exhortation to submission and obedience.

5

Epilogue: Proceed with Caution ...

Ever since posthumously converting Paul to Christianity, his interpreters have kept up a long tradition of transforming him into a Christian theologian and his letter to the Roman congregation into his *summa theologica*. That tradition persists in the West today, because it fits the historic model of a secularism that sequesters religion from the public, social, and political space by confining Paul to the private realm of personal piety (Cavanaugh 1995; Asad 2003: 21–66). Stripped of body, ethnic identity, social affiliation, and political relevance, a disembodied and deracialized Paul is now ready for co-optation by the powers that be. A case in point is the claim made by white American Evangelicals that 'conversion experiences fundamentally transcend barriers of race and class' (Scriven 2014: 263). So we have this incongruent picture that 'Christianity is acculturated and mixed with whiteness but presented in the society as meta-cultural and imperceptibly free from racialized entrapments' (Scriven 2014: 258; both citations in Park 2016: 220–1). Darryl Scriven's point is made about American Evangelicalism in particular but is applicable to most traditional interpretations of Paul as well.

The reading of Romans proposed in this volume takes its starting point in an embodied Paul, whose personal experiences are intimately tied to his identity as a diasporic Jew living as a colonized subject in the Roman Empire. While he should and can never be reduced to his environment, his identity cannot be understood apart from his ancestral traditions or his theology apart from the 'unceasing grief' he feels for his kinsfolk (Rom. 9.2).

Nor, for that matter, could his thoughts on such issues as law and justice, grace and faith, authorities and taxation be heard without taking account of the imperial propaganda to which he and his audience are subjected daily. Is it possible to abstract the hulking presence of Caesar and his religion, which permeates all facets of life and thought and which demands total allegiance from all Roman subjects, from Paul's command not '[to be] conformed to this age' (12.2)? In the course of answering these questions, we discover that from the start Paul engages Roman ideology and propaganda directly by speaking and acting self-consciously as an apocalyptic Jew deeply invested in the reconstitution of his own people. Like other apocalyptists of his day, Paul nurses fervent expectations for a reign of righteousness that promises to sweep aside all temporal regimes while recalling the people of the covenant from the four corners of the world. After these expectations have been repeatedly frustrated by failed uprisings and by corrupt rulers like the Hasmoneans and the Herods, Paul's apocalyptic hopes are jolted awake by Christ's resurrection. If Christ has indeed been raised, God's reign and justice will surely be established imminently and the elect will be delivered from enemy hands. If anyone is found to be in Christ, goes Paul's reasoning, the new creation must have been started and the final reckoning cannot be far off (2 Cor. 5.17).

What sets Paul apart from his fellow apocalyptists is his conviction that Gentiles must be included as part of the elect if this Jewish messiah is to become a cosmic Son of God (1.4). To transform a local leader into universal rulership, Paul recasts his universalism in the ethnic terms first popularized by the Greeks before being adopted by the Romans. He codeswitches from the imperial division between Greeks and barbarians to a division of humanity between Jews and Gentiles (1.14, 16). The reformulation gives priority to his kinsfolk but also gestures towards inclusion of erstwhile enemies into Ideal Israel. In using the master's tool, however, Paul also adopts Roman ethnic reasoning into his thinking. Inasmuch as Roman ethnography encodes an entitlement to universal rulership, Paul likewise claims his entitlement to universality. The Roman mandate is predicated on naming others as inferior barbarians in the same manner Nazi-sympathizer Carl Schmitt argues for distinguishing friends and enemies (Schmitt 2007: 25–7). Both are fundamental to the formation of nationalism. The existence and continual success of the Roman imperium depend on identifying enemies of the states; it cannot assert its superiority unless the barbarians are defined as inferior and in need of civilization. Paul's understanding of universality is cut from the same cloth. For his Jewish messiah to make his universal claim on the world and for his preaching of the good news to supersede the good news of the Caesar-religion, Gentiles must be included. Hence his eagerness to preach the good news in Rome (1.15) and to the ends of the earth (15.24, 28). The incorporation of Gentiles into the ranks of God's elect is therefore a crucial step in the development of Paul's political theology. Acceptance of Gentiles into the ancient covenant gives Ideal Israel the intellectual legitimacy to challenge the mighty empire of Rome.

In learning to use the master's tools, has Paul learned to use them too well? Has he replaced one form of universalism (*Pax Romana*) with another (*Pax Judaica*)? The proposal here is an improvement over supersessionism of all forms, which pit Christian universalism against the supposed ethnocentrism of Judaism (for critique, see Horrell 2017: 124–9), because Paul did not set out to start a new religion and could not have a notion of 'Christianity' or 'church', as we understand both terms today. And, as stressed throughout this book, there is no evidence in Romans or anywhere else in his letters that Paul intends the messianic community to be a replacement of Physical or Ideal Israel. The strategy with which Ideal Israel is formed is to extend the boundaries that separate Jews from Gentiles outwards until they encompass 'the fullness of Gentiles' when 'all Israel will be saved' (11.25). Because the inclusion of Gentiles into the covenant so radically redefines his ethnic categories, the only way for modern interpreters to resolve the confusion is to evaluate at every turn such terms as 'Jew', 'Gentile', and 'Israel'. At this point it may be helpful to remember that the Greek *ethnos* has a wide range of meanings from 'guild' to 'nation' to 'people' and every type of grouping in between and that the modern concept of ethnicity is based both on genetics and on social construction (Wan 2009: 130–4).

Nevertheless, any time universalism is invoked in the articulation of a religious movement, it opens itself up to co-optation by those who dominate, if not monopolize, the production of knowledge and, with that, the instruments of power. A convincing case has been made, for example, that a vision of universality has contributed to a de-racialized interpretation of the Bible that turns out to favour those who purport to speak not for their ethnic group but for all humanity (Bailey, Liew, & Segovia 2009; Horrell 2017; Park 2017). Because members of the dominant culture are able to submerge, unconsciously or by design, their own interpretation – particularized by class, race, ethnicity – under the cover of universality, their unexamined biases are then passed on as normalized, value-free, neutral values applicable to all peoples at all times across all ethnic and racial lines. Is Paul's universalism in danger of falling prey to such forces?

There are two safeguards against this danger. The first is Paul's conception of the peace of Christ, which, unlike the peace of Rome, is founded not on conquest and violence but on the self-sacrificial death of its leader. This irony of life through death, victory through defeat suffuses the guiding principles and all aspects of the New Community. The existence of the Community is possible in the first place because of a unique act of reconciliation – the Son of God reconciling the enemies to God by dying for them (5.6–11). The upside-down peace that results therefrom resists all forms of dominations and co-optation. In turn, the self-sacrificial peace makes it possible to form a community without borders by erasing the distinction between friends and enemies, by loving and feeding those outside our borders, that is, by putting into practice an inside-out love (12.3–9). The New Community must foreground these founding principles with vigilance for the sake of resisting the impulse for empire-building.

The second safeguard against destructive universalism is Paul's insistence on preserving the individuality of the New Community (12.3–8). In Romans Paul presents the body of Christ as a collective of diverse, distinct acts and gifts that cannot be homogenized into a unitary whole. Different members must be allowed to practice whatever gifts (*charismata*) they are given (12.6–8). The underlying principle here is the recognition that the community is made up of *both* Jews *and* Gentiles. Even though Paul's use of ethnic categories can be confusing in places, he is clear that Gentiles should remain Gentiles and Jews should remain Jews. While life together between the two groups can be a challenge, as events unfolded a few years earlier in Antioch (Gal. 2.11–14) can attest to, Paul has never advocated homogenization as a goal for the New Community. If anything, his well-known dictum of being all things to all people (1 Cor. 9.22) points in the opposite direction. Still, these guardrails are far from guarantees. The danger of Pauline universalism remains alive and well; abuses of all kinds have been perpetrated in the name of the apostle throughout history. The only solution is to warn all students of Paul, 'Proceed with caution…'.

Works Cited

Asad, Talal (2003), *Formations of the Secular: Christianity, Islam, Modernity* (Stanford: Stanford University Press).

Aus, Roger D. (1979), 'Paul's Travel Plans to Spain and the "Full Number of the Gentiles" of Rom. xi.25'. *Novum Testamentum* 21: 232–62.

Bailey, Randall, Tat-siong Liew, and Fernando Segovia (2009), 'Toward Minority Biblical Criticism: Framework, Contours, Dynamics', in R. Bailey, T.-s. Liew, and F. Segovia, eds., *They were all Together in One Place? Toward Minority Biblical Criticism* (Atlanta: Society of Biblical Literature), 3–46.

Balsdon, J. P. V. D. (1979), *Romans and Aliens* (London: Duckworth).

Barclay, John M. G. (1998), 'Paul and Philo on Circumcision: Romans 2.25–9 in Social and Cultural Context'. *New Testament Studies* 44: 536–66.

Barth, Karl (1933), *The Epistle to the Romans*. 6th ed., Trans. E. C. Hoskyns (London: Oxford).

Barth, Karl (1939), *Church and State*. Trans. G. R. Howe (London: SCMP; German original published in 1938).

Bassler, Jouette (1982), *Divine Impartiality and a Theological Axiom* (Chicago: Scholars Press).

Bauer, W., W. F. Arndt, F. W. Gingrich, and F. W. Danker (2000), *A Greek-English Lexicon of the New Testament and Other Early Christian Literature*. 3rd ed. (Chicago: University of Chicago Press).

Beyer, Hermann (1964), '*diakoneō*, etc', *Theological Dictionary of the New Testament* (Grand Rapids: Eerdmans) 2:81–93.

Blumenfeld, Bruno (2001), *The Political Paul: Justice, Democracy and Kingship in a Hellenistic Framework*, JSNT Supplement 210 (Sheffield: Sheffield Academic Press).

Boesak, Allan A. (1986), 'What Belongs to Caesar? Once Again Romans 13', in A. A. Boesak and C. Villa-Vicencio, eds., *When Prayer Makes News* (Philadelphia: Westminster), 138–57.

Bonhoeffer, Dietrich (1959), *The Cost of Discipleship*. Rev. ed., Trans. R. H. Fuller (New York: Macmillan).

Brown, Michael J. (2004), 'Paul's Use of δοῦλος Χρθστιῦ Ἰησοῦ in Romans 1:1'. *Journal of Biblical Literature* 120: 725–8.

Brunt, P. A. (1971), *Italian Manpower, 225 B.C. – A.D. 14* (Oxford: Clarendon Press).

Burns, Patout (2012), *Romans: Interpreted by Early Christian Commentators.* The Church's Bible. Grand Rapids: Eerdmans.

Burton, G. (1987), 'Government and the Provinces', in J. Wacher, ed., *The Roman World, Vol. I* (London & New York: Routledge).

Byrd, John P. (2013), *Sacred Scripture, Sacred War: The Bible and the American Revolution* (Oxford & New York: Oxford University Press).

Cavanaugh, William (1995), '"Fire Strong Enough to Consume the House": The Wars or Religion and the Rise of the State'. *Modern Theology* 11: 397–420.

Cohen, Shaye (1999), *Beginnings of Jewishness: Boundaries, Varieties, Uncertainties* (Berkeley: University of California Press).

Collins, John J. (1995), *The Scepter and the Star: The Messiahs of the Dead Sea Scrolls and Other Ancient Literature* (New York: Doubleday).

Conzelmann, H. 1974 'Chairō, Etc'. in *Theological Dictionary of the New Testament, Volume 9* (Grand Rapids: Eerdmans), 359–76.

de Jonge, Marinus (1994), 'Christ', *Anchor Yale Bible Dictionary* (New York: Doubleday). 1.914–21.

Delling, G. (1972a), 'tassō, etc'. *Theological Dictionary of the New Testament* (Grand Rapids: Eerdmans) 8: 27–48.

Delling, G. (1972b), 'hyperechō, hyperochē'. *Theological Dictionary of the New Testament* (Grand Rapids: Eerdmans) 8: 523.

Deissmann, Gustav Adolf (1964), *Light from the Ancient East*. Trans. L. R. Strachan (Grand Rapids: Baker).

Dittenberger, Wilhelm, ed. (1970), *Orientis Graeci inscriptiones selectae: Supplementum Sylloges inscriptionum Graecarum*. Two volumes (New York: Olms).

Dodd, C. H. (1959), *Epistle of Paul to the Romans* (London: Fontana Books).

Dunn, James D. G. (1986), 'Romans 13.1-7 – A Charter for Political Quietism?' *Ex auditu* 2: 55–68

Dunn, James D. G. (1988a), *Romans 1-8*. Word Bible Commentary (Dallas: Word Books).

Dunn, James D. G. (1988b), *Romans 9-16*. Word Bible Commentary (Dallas: Word Books).

Dunn, James D. G. (1998), *The Theology of Paul the Apostle* (Grand Rapids: Eerdmans).

Eisenbaum, Pamela (2009), *Paul was not a Christian: The Original Message of a Misunderstood Apostle* (New York: HarperCollins).

Elliott, Neil (1990), *The Rhetoric of Romans: Argumentative Constraints and Strategy and Paul's Dialogue with Judaism*. JSNT Supplement Series 45 (Sheffiedl: Sheffield Academic Press).

Elliott, Neil (1994), *Liberating Paul: The Justice of God and the Politics of the Apostle* (Maryknoll: Orbis).

Elliott, Neil (1997a), 'The Anti-Imperial Message of the Cross', in R. A. Horsley, ed., *Paul and Empire: Religion and Power in Roman Imperial Society* (Harrisburg: Trinity Press International), 167–83.

Elliott, Neil (1997b), 'Romans 13: 1–7 in the Context of Imperial Propaganda', in R. A. Horsley, ed., *Paul and Empire: Religion and Power in Roman Imperial Society* (Harrisburg: Trinity Press International), 184–204.

Elliott, Neil (2000), 'Paul and the Politics of Empire: Problems and Prospects', in R. A. Horsley, ed., *Paul and Politics: Ekklesia, Israel, Imperium, Interpretation* (Harrisburg, PA: Trinity Press International), 17–39.

Elliott, Neil (2008), *The Arrogance of Nations: Reading Romans in the Shadow of Empire* (Minneapolis: Fortress).

Feldman, Louis (1993), *Jew and Gentile in the Ancient World* (Princeton: Princeton University Press).

Fitzmyer, Joseph (1993), *Romans: A New Translation with Introduction and Commentary*, Anchor Bible (New York: Doubleday).

Foerster, W. (1964), '*Exestin*, etc', *Theological Dictionary of the New Testament* (Grand Rapids: Eerdmans) 2: 560–75.

Fridrichsen, Anton (1947), *The Apostle and His Message* (Uppsala: Lundequistska).

Friedrich, G. (1964), '*Euangelizomai, etc*'. *Theological Dictionary of the New Testament*. Grand Rapids: Eerdmans 2: 707–37.

Furnish, Victor P. (1979), *The Moral Teaching of Paul* (Nashville: Abingdon).

Gaventa, Beverly (2017), 'Reading Romans 13 with Simone Weil: Toward a More Generous Hermeneutic'. *JBL* 136: 7–22.

Gehrz, Chris (2017), 'Mike Pence, "Orientation to Authority," and Public Uses of Romans 13'. *Anxious Bench* (30 May) https://www.patheos.com/blogs/anxiousbench/2017/05/mike-pence-romans-13/; accessed 31 October 2018.

Georgi, Dieter (1991), *Theocracy in Paul's Praxis and Theology* (Minneapolis: Fortress Press).

Georgi, Dieter (1997), 'Who is the True Prophet', in R. A. Horsley, ed., *Paul and Empire: Religion and Power in Roman Imperial Society* (Harrisburg: Trinity Press International), 36–46.

Hall, Jonathan M. (1997), *Ethnic Identity in Greek Antiquity* (Cambridge: Cambridge University Press).

Harrison, James R. (2011), *Paul and the Imperial Authorities at Thessalonica and Rome: A Study in the Conflict of Ideology*. WUNT 273 (Tübingen: Mohr Siebeck).

Hassall, Mark (1987), 'Romans and Non-Romans', in J. Wacher, ed., *The Roman World, Vol. II* (London & New York: Routledge), 685–700.

Hays, Richard B. (1985), '"Have We Found Abraham to Be Our Forefather According to the Flesh?" A Reconsideration of Rom. 4:1'. *Novum Testamentum* 27: 76–98.

Hecht, R. D. (1984), 'The Exegetical Contexts of Philo's Interpretation of Circumcision', in F. E. Greenspahn et al., eds., *Nourished with Peace* (Chicago: Scholars Press), 51–79.

Herzog, William (1994), 'Dissembling, A Weapon of the Weak: The Case of Christ and Caesar in Mark 12: 13–17and Romans 13:1–7'. *Perspectives in Religious Studies* 21: 339–60.

Horrell, David (2017), 'Paul, Inclusion and Whiteness: Particularizing Interpretation'. *Journal for the Study of the New Testament* 40 (2): 123–47.

Horsley, Richard A. (1987), *Jesus and the Spiral of Violence* (San Francisco: Harper and Row).

Hurtado, Larry (1998), *One God, One Lord: Early Christian Devotion and Ancient Jewish Monotheism*. 2nd ed. (Edinburgh: T&T Clark).

Jewett, Robert (1993), 'Tenement Churches and Communal Meals in the Early Church: The Implications of a Form-Critical Analysis of 2 Thess 3:10'. *Biblical Research* 38: 23–43.

Jewett, Robert (2004), 'The Corruption and Redemption of Creation: Reading Rom. 8: 18–23 within the Context of Imperial Context', in R. A. Horsley, ed., *Paul and the Roman Imperial Order* (Harrisburg: Trinity Press International), 25–46.

Jewett, Robert (2006), *Romans*, Hermeneia (Minneapolis: Fortress Press).

Kallas, James (1965), 'Romans 13:1–7: An Interpolation'. *New Testament Studies* 11: 365–74.

Käsemann, Ernst (1969a), 'Principles of the Interpretation of Romans 13', in *New Testament Questions of Today* (Philadelphia: Fortress), 196–216.

Käsemann, Ernst (1969b), 'The Righteousness of God in Paul', in *New Testament Questions of Today* (Philadelphia: Fortress), 168–82.

Käsemann, Ernst (1980), *Commentary on Romans*. Trans. G. W. Bromiley (Grand Rapids: Eerdmans).

Keener, Craig (2009), *Romans: A New Covenant Commentary* (Eugene, OR: Cascade).

Kidd, Thomas (2014), 'Does the Bible Prohibit Revolution'. *Anxious Bench* (14 October) https://www.patheos.com/blogs/anxiousbench/2014/10/does-the-bible-prohibit-revolution/; accessed 28 October 2018.

Koester, Helmut (1997), 'Imperial Ideology and Paul's Eschatology in I Thessalonians', in R. A. Horsley, ed., *Paul and Empire: Religion and Power in Roman Imperial Society* (Harrisburg: Trinity Press International), 158–66.

Kraft, Dina (2018), 'The Real Story behind the Nazi Establishment's Use of "Romans 13."' *Haaretz* (19 June) https://www.haaretz.com/us-news/.premium-the-real-story-behind-the-nazi-establishment-s-use-of-romans-13-1.6194455; accessed 31 October 2018.

Lampe, Peter (1992), 'Prisca', in *Anchor Bible Dictionary* (New York: Doubleday), 5.467–68.

Lampe, Peter (2003), *From Paul to Valentinus: Christians at Rome in the First Two Centuries*. Trans. M. Steinhauser (Minneapolis: Fortress).

Landes, P. F., ed. (1982), *Augustine on Romans* (Chicago: Scholars Press).

Lehman, Paul (1975), *The Transfiguration of Politics* (New York: Harper & Row).

Liddell, H. G., Robert Scott, and H. S. Jones (1968), *A Greek-English Lexicon*. Rev. ed. (Oxford: At the Clarendon Press).

Long, Colleen (2018), 'Sessions Cites Bible to Defend Separating Immigrant Families'. *AP News* (14 June) https://apnews.com/0bcc5d5d077247769da065 864d215d1b; accessed 31 October 2018.

Longenecker, Richard (2016), *The Epistle to the Romans: A Commentary on the Greek Text*. The New International Greek Testament Commentary (Grand Rapids: Eerdmans).

Mullen, Lincoln (2018), 'The Fight to Define Romans 13'. *The Atlantic* (15 June) https://www.theatlantic.com/ideas/archive/2018/06/romans-13/562916/; accessed 31 October 2018.

Munck, Johannes (1959), *Paul and the Solvation of Mankind*. Trans. F. Clarke (Richmond: John Knox).

Myers-Scotton, Carol (1993), *Social Motivations for Codeswitching: Evidence from Africa* (Oxford: Clarendon).

Noll, Mark (2006), *The Civil War as a Theological Crisis* (Chapel Hill: University of North Carolina Press).

Noll, Mark (2016), *In the Beginning Was the Word: The Bible in American Public Life, 1492–1783* (New York & Oxford: Oxford University Press).

O'Collins, Gerald G. (1994), 'Crucifixion', *Anchor Yale Bible Dictionary* (New York: Doubleday). 1.1207–10.

Park, Wongi (2016), 'Christological Discourse as Racial Discourse'. *Religion & Theology* 23: 213–30.

Park, Wongi (2017), 'The Black Jesus, the Mestizo Jesus, and the Historical Jesus'. *Biblical Interpretation* 25: 190–205.

Pence, Mike (2017), 'Remarks by the Vice President at the US Naval Academy Commencement Ceremony'. Whitehouse.gov 26 May 2017 (https://www.whitehouse.gov/briefings-statements/remarks-vice-president-us-naval-academy-commencement-ceremony/; accessed 5 November 2018).

Porter, Stanley (1990), 'Romans 13: 1–7 as Pauline Political Rhetoric', *Filologia neotestamentaria* 3: 115–37.

Price, S. R. F. (1997), 'Rituals and Power', in R. A. Horsley, ed., *Paul and Empire: Religion and Power in Roman Imperial Society* (Harrisburg: Trinity Press International), 47–71.

Roetzel, Calvin J. (2000), 'Response: How Anti-Imperial Was the Collection and How Emancipatory Was Paul's Project', in R. A. Horsley, ed., *Paul and Politics: Ekklesia, Israel, Imperium, Interpretation* (Harrisburg: Trinity Press International), 227–30.

Sanders, E. P. (1977), *Paul and Palestinian Judaism: A Comparison of Patterns of Religion* (Philadelphia: Fortress).

Schmitt, Carl (2007), *The Concept of the Political*. Trans. G. Schwab. Expanded ed. (Chicago: University of Chicago Press).

Schüssler Fiorenza, Elisabeth (1988), 'The Ethics of Biblical Interpretation: Decentering Biblical Scholarship'. *Journal of Biblical Literature* 107: 3–17

Scott, James C. (1985), *Weapons of the Weak: Everyday Forms of Peasant Resistance* (New Haven: Yale University Press).

Scott, James C. (1990), *Domination and the Arts of Resistance: Hidden Transcripts* (New Haven: Yale University Press).

Scriven, Darryl (2014), 'Theological Afterward: The Call to Blackness in American Christianity', in J. R. Hawkins and P. L. Sinitiere, eds., *Christianity and the Color Line: Race and Religion after Divided by Faith* (Oxford: Oxford University Press), 255–74.

Segal, Alan F. (1990), *Paul the Convert: The Apostolate and Apostasy of Saul the Pharisee* (New Haven: Yale University Press).

Stanley, Christopher (1996), '"Neither Jew nor Greek": Ethnic Conflict in Graeco-Roman Society'. *Journal for the Study of the New Testament* 64: 101–24,

Stendahl, Krister (1976), 'The Apostle Paul and the Introspective Conscience of the West', in *Paul among Jews and Gentiles and Other Essays* (Philadelphia: Fortress), 78–96. Originally published in 1964.

Stendahl, Krister (1995), *Final Account: Paul's Letter to the Romans* (Minneapolis: Fortress).

Stowers, Stanley (1994), *Reading Romans: Justice, Jews, and Gentiles* (New Haven: Yale University Press).

Stein, Robert H. (1989), 'The Argument of Romans 13:1–7'. *Novum Testamentum* 31: 332–6.

Strathmann, H. and R. Meyer (1967), '*Leitourgeō*, etc'. *Theological Dictionary of the New Testament* 4: 231.

Strobel, Adolf (1956), 'Zum Verständnis von Röm 13'. *Zeitschrift für die neutestamentliche Wissenschaft* 47: 67–93.

Sumney, Jerry (2007), 'Paul and Christ-Believing Jews Whom He Opposes', in Jackson-McCabe, ed., *Jewish Christianity Reconsidered: Rethinking Ancient Groups and Texts* (Minneapolis: Fortress), 57–80.

Tannehill, Robert (1967), *Dying and Rising with Christ: A Study in Pauline Theology* (Berlin: Töpelmann).

Taubes, Jacob (2004), *Political Theology of Paul*. Trans. D. Hollander (Stanford: Stanford University Press).

Thorsteinsson, Runar M. (2003), *Paul's Interlocutor in Romans 2: Function and Identity in the Context of Ancient Epistolography*. Coniectanea biblica New Testament Series 40 (Stockholm: Almqvist & Wiksell International).

von Lehndorff, Hans Graf (1961), *Ostpreussisches Tagebuch: Aufzeichnungen eines Arztes aus den Jahren 1945–1947*, 13th ed. (Munich: Biederstein).

Wan, Sze-kar (2000a), 'Collection for the Saints as Anti-Colonial Act: Implications of Paul's Ethnic Reconstruction', in R. A. Horsley, ed., *Paul and Politics: Ekklesia, Israel, Imperium, Interpretation* (Harrisburg: Trinity Press International), 191–215.

Wan, Sze-kar (2000b), *Power in Weakness: Conflict and Rhetorics in Paul's Second Letter to the Corinthians* (The New Testament in Context; Valley Forge: Trinity Press International).

Wan, Sze-kar (2008), 'Coded Resistance: A Proposed Rereading of Romans 13: 1–7', in C. B. Kittredge et al., ed., *The Bible in the Public Square* (Minneapolis: Augsburg/Fortress Press), 173–84.

Wan, Sze-kar (2009), '"To the Jew First and Also to the Greek": Reading Romans as Ethnic Construction', in E. Schüssler Fiorenza and L. Nasrallah, ed., *Prejudice and Christian Beginnings: Investigating Race, Gender, and Ethnicity in Early Christianity* (Minneapolis: Augsburg/Fortress), 129–55.

Weber, Thomas (2018), 'When Romans 13 Was Invoked to Justify Evil'. *CNN* (22 June) https://www.cnn.com/2018/06/22/opinions/jeff-sessions-bible-verse-nazi-germany-opinion-weber/index.html; accessed 24 July 2018.

White, John L. (1999), *The Apostle of God: Paul and the Promise of Abraham* (Peabody: Henrickson).

Wiefel, Wolfgang (1991), 'Jewish Community in Ancient Rome and the Origins of Roman Christianity', in K. P. Donfried, ed., *The Romans Debate* (Rev. & expanded; Peabody: Hendrickson), 85–101.

Winter, Bruce (1994), *Seek the Welfare of the City: Christians as Benefactors and Citizens* (Grand Rapids: Eerdmans).

Wright, N. T. (2013), *Paul and the Faithfulness of God* (Minneapolis: Fortress.

Index